I'M
FASCINATED
BY
SACRIFICE
FLIES

Also by Tim Kurkjian

America's Game
Is This a Great Game, or What?

I'M FASCINATED BY SACRIFICE FLIES

Inside the Game We All Love

TIM KURKJIAN

FOREWORD BY GEORGE F. WILL

 ST. MARTIN'S GRIFFIN 🐏 NEW YORK

The Library of Congress has cataloged the hardcover edition as follows:

Names: Kurkjian, Tim, author.
Title: I'm fascinated by sacrifice flies : inside the game we all love / Tim Kurkjian ;
foreword by George F. Will.
Description: New York, N.Y. : St. Martin's Press, 2016.
Identifiers: LCCN 2015048747|ISBN 9781250077936 (hardcover) |
ISBN 9781466890275 (e-book)
Subjects: LCSH: Baseball—United States. | Baseball—United States—Miscellanea. |
BISAC: SPORTS & RECREATION / Baseball / Essays & Writings.
Classification: LCC GV863.A1 K874 2016 | DDC 796.3570973—dc23
LC record available at http://lccn.loc.gov/2015048747

ISBN 978-1-250-12989-5 (trade paperback)

First St. Martin's Griffin Edition: May 2017

10 9 8 7 6 5 4 3 2 1

TO **KATHY, KELLY,** AND **JEFF**.
THANKS FOR ALL THE SUPPORT.
THANKS FOR ENCOURAGING ME TO
WRITE ANOTHER BOOK.

Contents

Foreword

TIM KURKJIAN BEGINS this delightfully informative and entertaining stroll down baseball's broad, sunlit boulevard by recounting how he once astonished colleagues on ESPN's *Baseball Tonight* by exclaiming on the air, "I'm fascinated by sacrifice flies!" Was he—is he—eccentric? Not at all. When you read chapter seven, you will understand how this seemingly simple part of baseball offense can seize the imagination of one of the game's most enthusiastic and diligent chroniclers.

Do you know who has held, for more than half a century, the record for hitting the most sacrifice flies in a season? You soon will. Do you know that you can get credit for a sacrifice fly while hitting into a double play? Tim tells you how.

He derives more fun from his vocation than anyone I know. He knows, however, that baseball is not always fun for those who play it.

The word *fear* is the entire first paragraph of the first chapter of an insufficiently remembered baseball book from more than fifty years ago. It is Leonard Koppett's *A Thinking Man's Guide to Baseball*. Koppett's startlingly abrupt beginning to his book was

his way of forcing fans to shed some of the obscuring sentimen-
tality that sometimes envelops baseball. He wanted them to face a
fact from which they often flinch.

Sentimentalists may speak of ballplayers as "boys of summer"
but in fact they are men, and their work is dangerous. They are,
as Tim says, "hard men playing a hard game." When a six-ounce
baseball comes hurtling out of a pitcher's hand approximately 55
feet from home plate, the batter has about .28 seconds, give or take
a few hundredths of a second, to decide whether the pitch will be
a ball or a strike—or a mortal danger. Tim quotes Kevin Seitzer's
description of being hit in the face by a Scott Erickson pitch in
1995: "It was like my face was crushed by a bowling ball, a bowling ball going 95 mph."

Baseball, Tim persuasively argues, is not only dangerous, it is
the most difficult game to play. "There are," he says, "more two-
and three-sport high school athletes playing in the major leagues
than there are in the NBA, NFL, or NHL." The Mets third baseman David Wright says, "I would say that most Major League
Baseball players don't sleep well at night. The game is too hard."
Tim lets a player tell you just how hard it is: "Reds center fielder
Billy Hamilton, who scored 22 touchdowns his senior year as a
receiver in high school, and averaged 27 points a game in hoops,
told me, 'Baseball is the hardest sport. Not even close. There are
nights in baseball where it looks like I've never played the game
before. That would never happen in the other sports. My athleticism would just take over.'"

How hard is it to hit a 95-mph fastball? As Tim says, Tiger
Woods can become incensed if a single camera click occurs during his backswing—and the ball he is trying to hit is not moving.
The crowd is asked to be quiet when a tennis player is about to
serve a ball he controls. "But when a hitter is trying to make con-

tact with Aroldis Chapman's 100-mph heater, the crowd is urged to go wild."

To reach the top in this demanding game requires extraordinary competitiveness, which manifests itself off the field as well as on it. J. J. Hardy, the Orioles' Gold Glove shortstop, has the astonishing athletic talents you would expect in someone whose mother played on the LPGA tour and whose father was a professional tennis player. J.J. is such a talented Ping-Pong player that, Tim says, one day in spring training a teammate beat him. And "Five minutes later, Hardy received a text from the Brewers' Ryan Braun, who was 2,500 miles away. It read: 'I heard you lost in Ping-Pong.'"

It is frequently said and always true that there is a lot of failure in baseball. There also can be—actually, there must be—a lot of humor in failure. "In the late 1980s," Tim writes, "Orioles outfielder Brady Anderson was a passenger in a car driven by teammate Rene Gonzales, who was going far too fast on a very dangerous road late at night in the rain. Anderson said to Gonzales, 'Gonz, if I wasn't hitting .178, I'd ask you to slow down.'"

This book is, among many other things, a guide to baseball's unwritten rules, unbelievable superstitions, and unexpected hilarities, one of which occurred when a coach new to the Milwaukee Brewers was asked to tell at a team meeting a highlight from his career as a player. The coach mentioned hitting a home run into the upper deck of old Tiger Stadium. Then-Brewers slugging first baseman Prince Fielder, whose father, Cecil, had played for the Tigers, piped up: "I did that when I was 12!"

Baseball, the game with the longest season and the longest reach into America's past, continually generates enchanting statistical oddities. Tim discerns them so that the rest of us can savor them. For example, pitcher Madison Bumgarner hit more grand slam home runs in a season (two) than Derek Jeter did in his career (one). And Babe Ruth, Willie Mays, Hank Aaron, and Barry Bonds never hit for the cycle, but Bengie Molina—who is extremely slow even by catchers' standards—did. Or the fact that Scott Sizemore, playing his first game at first base, participated in a triple play, something that Steve Garvey, Fred McGriff, Mark Grace, and Rafael Palmeiro never did in their combined 8,599 games playing first.

There is an old saying: If you love your work, you will never work a day in your life.

Tim's love for what he does is, happily, infectious. His aim with this book is to spread the happiness that baseball has given to him and can give to those who immerse themselves in its lore and complexities.

Elliot Johnson, a journeyman infielder, told Tim this story about how someone in the stands heckled him. The heckler yelled, "Elliot Johnson, Elliot Johnson, I Googled you, and the reply was, 'Why?'" Johnson says, "I turned and gave him the thumbs-up. That was pretty funny." Google Tim and, if Google has a lick of sense, its reply will be: "Tim Kurkjian is, of course, the base-ball commentator with the best stock of stories." If you doubt this, just turn this page and get on with the pleasure of getting to know the mind of the man who is fascinated by sacrifice flies.

—George F. Will

Introduction

STEVE BERTHIAUME WAS worried about me anyway. As one of the hosts of ESPN's *Baseball Tonight,* he had seen me clip box scores from the newspaper and tape them in my box score book, a daily ritual that, pathetically, I did for twenty years without missing a day. He had seen me keep a daily tally of all sorts of ridiculous statistics, including players that strike out four times in a game; every year, there are 100-plus, though Bill Buckner never struck out three times in a game. And Berthiaume was in the ESPN newsroom the night I leaped from my chair because something I'd been following every day for years had finally happened: the Angels' Garret Anderson was hit by a pitch for the first time in 5½ seasons. And Berthiaume was there when I incorrectly referred to the movie as *The Devil Wears Prado,* no doubt having much-traveled infielder Martin Prado on my mind, to which ESPN colleague Wendi Nix quickly corrected me, saying, "Tim, it's Prada, not Prado. *The Devil Wears Prada.* What is wrong with you?"

But on the night of July 1, 2007, Berthiaume had had enough of me and my baseball obsessions. The Astros' Carlos Lee had hit a sacrifice fly, his 13th of the season, which set the club record, and he wasn't even at the All-Star break. So, in a fit of excitement, and in another lack of clarity, I blurted out on *Baseball Tonight*, "I'm fascinated by sacrifice flies."

Berthiaume stopped the live broadcast and said, "Wait a minute! Did you just say you are fascinated by sacrifice flies?" That was followed by a minute of warranted chiding from Berthiaume and my fellow analysts Orel Hershiser and Eduardo Pérez. My comeback to them was even lamer than my declarative sentence. I shot back, "Stop making fun of me!"

I deserved it, but the fact is I'm fascinated by sacrifice flies. I am fascinated by so many aspects of baseball and, in this book, I'll attempt to show you from where my fascination comes, and where and how you can find it for yourself. In the wake of fading attendance and TV ratings, in the aftermath of the Steroid Era that stained the game for so many, in a time where so many players are so rich that they have a sense of entitlement that they haven't earned, I will show you how to love the game for the first time, or more than ever.

There are chapters in this book that have appeared on ESPN .com: Hit by Pitch, Sounds of the Game, Superstitions, and Unwritten Rules. They are among my favorite stories that I've ever written because I learned so much writing them and, hopefully, so will you. Adam LaRoche told me the pain in his knee was so fierce after being hit by a pitch, "I almost threw up." In Sounds of the Game, there are Jake Peavy's primal screams from the mound, and Adam Dunn talking to himself while playing first base. In Superstitions, there are Torii Hunter's perfectly shined shoes, and a poker chip in Sean Burnett's back pocket. In Unwritten Rules, imagine the reaction if a player texted while running around the bases after hitting a homer.

I will explain why baseball is the best game: Pete Rose taking batting practice only minutes after getting out of prison is one of my favorite new stories. I will explain why baseball is the hardest game to play: please, don't ever wear a watch while trying to catch Robb Nen. I will explain where I work, ESPN, and what it's like to sit alone with Buck Showalter in a room with games on fifteen TVs, and how he taught me to watch a game, what to look for when evaluating: never draft a player with bright blue eyes, or an 18-year-old with a full beard. I'll tell you about Terry Francona's one year on TV, from which I learned so much, and laughed so hard: one night in Philadelphia, his closer came into a game with mustard all over his uniform jersey. And I will tell you of the day when John Kruk randomly asked me, "Did I ever tell you about the time that I shot a deer in a hot tub?"

I will explain what the late Don Zimmer, Mike Flanagan, Earl Weaver, and Tony Gwynn meant to the game, and how they made the game so much more fun and interesting to watch: Gwynn nearly started to cry after breaking his favorite bat in 1995. I'll explain my fascination with names, and why, for hours, I pored over Barry Bonds's home run victims, 449 of them, including Abbott and Castillo, Dustin and Hoffman, Green and Bere. I will explain the beauty of the box score, and why I cut out every one of them for twenty years: 9-0-0-0-0-15 had never been seen before 2014, and likely will never be seen again.

I will explain what a Quirkjian is, and how to find them in box scores, at a game, or in *The Shawshank Redemption*. I will explain why strikeouts are so prevalent today: more hitters struck out 100 times in 2014 than in 1900–63 combined. I will explain the role of an official scorer: don't do that job, it is too hard. I will explain the future of the game, which remains bright as long as the Joe Maddons of the world are always taking an active role.

And, of course, I'll tell why *I'm Fascinated by Sacrifice Flies*.

I'M
FASCINATED
BY
SACRIFICE
FLIES

1. THE BEST GAME

I Put Aqua Net on My Glove

BASEBALL IS THE best game.

I knew that when I was 6 years old, and I know that better than ever at nearly 60. It is the best game for so many reasons: its degree of difficulty, its rich history and tradition, the odd, quirky results that it so often brings, the odd, quirky players that it so often produces, and the leisurely pace at which it is played, which allows us so much time to examine and dissect the diverse and important questions within a game.

"During the game tonight, while we were sitting on the bench," then-Braves center fielder B. J. Upton said to me after a game, "my brother [Justin] asked me, 'What size shoes do you think Tim wears?'"

"I wear a 7½," I said.

"Wow," he said, "that's really small."

It is the best game because almost every player, manager, and coach in the game is connected in some way, be it former teammates in A-ball at Bakersfield, or in winter ball in the Dominican, or part of this uncomfortable first-time meeting between a hitter and a catcher in the batter's box during a big-league game: "I fucked your cousin last week," the catcher said to the hitter. The shocked and appalled hitter said, "Cindy? You fucked Cindy?"

Former pitcher Steve Karsay is the common denominator for the Hall of Fame Class of 2014: managers Bobby Cox, Tony La Russa, and Joe Torre, and players Greg Maddux, Tom Glavine, and Frank Thomas. Karsay played for all three managers, and with all three players. "I didn't even know that," he said. And then there was the trip to Marlins camp on the ESPN Bus Tour in spring training 2011 when I asked my large, lovable friend John Kruk if he knew Marlins manager Edwin Rodriguez.

"Yeah, I picked up his teeth one day," Kruk said. "The last week of the [winter ball] season [in 1985], he turned the wrong way on a fastball and got hit in the mouth with a pitch. His teeth came flying out. I picked up his teeth and gave them to him."

Rodriguez could laugh about it twenty-six years later, saying, "José De León was our first-base coach that day. He came to home plate to see how I was doing after being hit. He saw all the blood pouring out of my mouth, and he fainted. They put him on a stretcher and took him away in an ambulance. They didn't take me."

It is the best game because of its unpredictability, which I learned again in the 2014 postseason when I went 0 for 9 in predictions. Nine postseason matchups, including the two Wild Card games, and I got them all wrong: 0 for 9. One of my colleagues at ESPN, Jim Bowden, a former general manager of the Reds and Nationals, was, like me, 0 for 8 heading into the World Series. I picked the Royals, he picked the Giants. "The loser is the worst," Bowden told me. The Giants beat the Royals in seven. So officially, I was the worst.

I am not proud or happy about going 0 for 9, but I will not apologize for it because it only proves my point: the game is too great for anyone to predict it or understand it. If we actually had any idea what was going to happen, baseball would be the NBA. I love basketball, I love the NBA, but we knew before the 2013–14 season that the Heat was going to play the Pacers in the Eastern Conference Finals, and that's precisely what happened. But in baseball, we don't know what will happen from year to year, game to game, moment to moment.

And that is its special appeal. LeBron James dominates every game. One way or another, he is always the best player on the court; he touches the ball on every possession. Michael Jordan, Larry Bird, and Kobe Bryant always take the last shot. There is little chance that the last man on an NBA team is even in the game for the final seconds, and there's no chance that he will take the last shot. But in baseball, the 25th guy can be the hero; he can be Larry Bird for a night, for the biggest night. Ex-Cardinals third baseman David Freese quit baseball after high school, went to college as a regular student, decided to play ball again, then ten years later, hit a home run in the eleventh inning to win Game 6 of the 2011 World Series, perhaps the most remarkable game of the 3,500 or so that I have seen in person. When the Cardinals trailed by two runs in the tenth inning, after having tied the score with two in the ninth, I told my producer, Shawn Fitzgerald, if the Cardinals won the game that night, I'd never watch another baseball game because nothing could top this game.

Another lesson learned: the game always tops itself; it never disappoints, if you're paying attention. Freese joined a long list of unsung players in baseball history that, from nowhere, took the last shot and won the game. Marco Scutaro of the Giants was that guy in 2012, a little journeyman second baseman silently acquired from the Rockies in late July. He somehow helped carry the Giants into October, and became a World Series hero. On a different level, the Giants' Madison Bumgarner, a very good pitcher, became a combination of Sandy Koufax, Christy Mathewson, and Walter Johnson in the postseason, dominating October while the best pitcher in the game, Clayton Kershaw, got shelled. Such things can't happen in basketball. LeBron can't be held to seven a game in the conference finals—it's impossible. In baseball, anything is possible.

It is the best game because heroes in baseball come in all shapes and sizes. Marlins right fielder Giancarlo Stanton, who in November 2014 signed the biggest contract in American sports history—thirteen years, $325 million—is the biggest, strongest baseball player I have ever seen, and hits the ball to places that no one in the game ever has. He is 6′5″, 250 pounds, has a 34-inch waist, and he can really run.

"He hit the genetic jackpot," said former teammate Greg Dobbs. "I'd like to look like him for one day."

When I asked Stanton if his parents are also big and athletic, he said his dad is "a normal-looking guy, maybe 6 foot, gray hair."

So normal, in fact, that former Marlins teammate Bryan Peterson once asked Stanton, "Who is that old guy that I see following you around all the time? Is that some sycophant?"

Stanton laughed and said, "No, that's my dad!" As for his mom, Stanton looked at me (I'm 5′5″), and said, "My mom is almost as short as you!" Almost.

The Rangers' Prince Fielder is 5′9″, weighs 275, looks nothing like Stanton, but "he is the strongest man in baseball," said former teammate Ryan Braun. "And I really believe if he entered the World's Strongest Man competition—you know, carrying logs on his back—he would hold his own."

Former teammate Casey McGehee said, "He is so strong, he

doesn't even swing hard to hit a ball out of the ballpark. The rest of us are blowing snot bubbles just to get it over the fence."

Fielder's arms are so big, said former teammate Rich Donnelly, "You could put a tattoo of the United States on one bicep, and still have room for Argentina."

Fielder, when he played for the Tigers, once showed his teammates a video of him wrestling a professional sumo wrestler from Japan. "It was unbelievable," said former teammate Phil Coke. "Prince just chucked the guy across the room."

And then there is pitcher Loek Van Mil, who played minor league baseball for the Twins and Angels, but never made it to the big leagues, which is a shame because he is 7'1", from the Netherlands, and didn't play basketball as a kid because it wasn't offered in his school in Holland. He said he gets asked "ten or fifteen times a day" if he is a basketball player.

"I've played some pickup basketball," he said. Asked if he can dunk, he said, "Yes. I only need a 6-inch vertical. White men can't jump, but I can jump 6 inches." Van Mil was a catcher until he was 14, when he was 6'6". "I got a little too big to be a catcher," he said. "Shin guards are supposed to cover the tip of your toes, but they only covered my ankles. That's why I quit catching." His teammates loved him because he is the tallest player in the history of pro ball, he's funny, and he'd ride his bike to the ballpark. He laughed and said, "A lady stopped her car once and said, 'You're too big to ride a bike.'"

Tall or short, the common denominator of every baseball player is strong hands, and no one's hands are stronger than those of the Cardinals' Matt Holliday. "When I signed with the Cardinals, for my physical, I had to take a hand-strength test," said outfielder Lance Berkman. "I had a very low score the first time so they asked me, 'Can you take it again?' I did. I scored low again, and the trainer said, 'For a guy with 300 home runs, you should have stronger hands.' I said, 'Sorry, this is all I got. But don't compare my hands to Albert Pujols's hands, or Matt Holliday's hands. His are stronger than Herman Munster's.'"

The Red Sox's Dustin Pedroia has really small hands. "It's like shaking hands with a seven-year-old," said former Red Sox manager Terry Francona.

Former Red Sox GM Theo Epstein said Pedroia's hands are the "smallest I've ever seen on a baseball player."

But those hands are really strong. Pedroia is 5′6½″ tops, an inch and a half taller than Astros second baseman Jose Altuve, who, in 2014, became the second player since Snuffy Stirnweiss in 1945 to lead his league in batting, hits, and stolen bases in the same season.

Royals reliever Tim Collins is 5′6½″ and throws 95 mph. In the 2014 World Series, he joined Bobby Shantz (5′6″) as the only pitchers under 5′7″ to appear in a World Series game. "People don't believe that I'm a major league player, then after I convince them, they think I'm a second baseman," Collins said. "I tell them that I'm a pitcher and they say, 'No way, you're too short.' I'm not. And I read a book about Bobby Shantz."

In spring training several years ago, I interviewed Collins back-to-back, sort of a height-off interview. "I've never won one of these," I said.

"Neither have I," Tim Collins said. "Until now."

The Giants' Tim Lincecum is closer to 5′11″, but with his shirt off, he looks like he's 14. "I went to high school at 4′11″," he said. "I was throwing about 85 [mph] then. Then I grew to about 5′2″. I was throwing 90 then. Then I went to 5′7″, and all of a sudden, I was throwing 95." Lincecum is further proof that the throwing of a baseball is a God-given skill: you either have it or you don't, and it doesn't matter what size you are. Daniel Herrera has it. He pitched for several teams. He's listed at 5′8″, but said he's 5′6″, 145 pounds.

"The first time I saw him was during the week of the Kentucky Derby, and we figured he would have to leave the team that Saturday to go ride one of the horses," said former outfielder Adam Dunn, who was Herrera's teammate for part of one season in Cincinnati. "I've never faced him. But I haven't faced anyone his size since I was 11 or 12 years old."

Herrera has heard all the short jokes.

"The best one was in 2010," he said. "I was at Louisville [AAA]. One of our catchers, Albert Colina, who is a really big guy, picked me up and put me in his lap as he sat in the bullpen. Then he stuck his arm inside my jacket, and up my back. He wouldn't let me go. I thought, 'What is he doing?' Then, whenever I would talk, he would move his lips. Everyone was cracking up. He was the ventriloquist, and I was the puppet. That was the best one."

It is the best game because the players are so competitive. I played in a charity golf tournament, a scramble, in January 2013 in Orlando. The group behind us included Tigers pitcher Justin Verlander, who was just over a year removed from winning the AL MVP and Cy Young, but this day was about golf, not baseball, and all he cared about was winning the tournament, and the longest-drive contest. At the turn, I asked him how his group was doing. "We're one under birdie," he said. "In a scramble, you should at least birdie every hole, so I never count under par, I count under birdie." They were 10 under par at the turn, and won at 23 under. Verlander won the long-drive, and twice on the back nine, he hit into our group while we were standing on the green of a *par four*. Each time we looked around to see who had hit a ball at least 350 yards off the tee, there was Justin Verlander leaping in the air, arms raised, as if he had won the World Series.

That is how he lives his life: everything is a competition, especially pitching, and no matter what it is, he has to win. In spring training every year, the Tiger pitchers run sprints, and Verlander *has* to win every sprint. As a kid, he said, he always had to finish dinner faster than anyone in the family. "Even now, I'll be walking next to someone on the sidewalk, and I have to walk faster than him," he said. "I don't know why. That's the way I am."

Cal Ripken Jr. is one of the most competitive people I've ever met in my life. I used to play basketball with him and his group. One night, the score was 14-14, game to 15 by ones. No one was waiting, just ten guys on a cold December night in a dingy little gym. Ripken called a time-out—in a pickup game!—to figure out how they were going to score the last basket. They missed, we rebounded, we scored, and he was furious. I went about fifteen years without playing with him again until 2002 when I was assigned to do a story on the gym he had built at his house. He insisted that I play in the games that night even though at 45, I was totally overmatched against a 23-year-old who just finished his career at a Division II school.

Ripken flipped the game ball to me and said, "This feels just like your ball." Not only did he remember that we had used my ball as the game ball fifteen years earlier, but he remembered *how it felt in his hands*. So, thanks mostly to me, our team lost all nine games that night, same 0–9 as my postseason predictions in 2014. That was the last time I played basketball with him, and ten years after that embarrassing night, our friend Rick Sutcliffe asked if I had really played basketball with Ripken. "Yes," Ripken said, "and the last time he played, his team went 0–9." Ten years after a random night of basketball, one of a thousand nights that he played, he remembered what my team had done. Why? It was a competition, it was about winning and losing, not just for him, but for everyone.

"Why would you remember the 0–9 that night?" I asked him.

"Why wouldn't I?" he said.

Nolan Ryan threw a baseball as hard as any man alive for twenty-five years, and was proud of that. So, at age 65, he was asked to throw out the first ball at a Rangers game. Ryan, being Ryan, was not about to just go out there and lob a pitch from the front of the mound. He got loose in the batting cage under the stadium, went to the top of the mound, and fired his ceremonial first pitch at about 80 mph to Jim Sundberg, a six-time Gold Glover. But he was not ready for 80 mph. "I barely caught it," Sundberg said. "I had to bend down quickly to catch it. I split my pants."

It is the best game because the players so value the equipment that they use, especially their gloves. Before a game at Fenway Park in 2012, I watched infielder Nick Punto, then with the Red Sox, playing catch. His glove appeared to be wet. I asked him what he had put on his glove. "Well, today," he said, "I put a little Aqua Net on it, and a little suntan lotion. I do that to keep it lubricated, but it can't be floppy, it has to be stiff. Almost anything on it will work. The other day, I was in the bathroom in the clubhouse, and I'm sitting on the toilet, and when I'm done, I picked up a can of Glade off the floor and sprayed it in the air. Then I thought, 'Maybe this will work.' So I sprayed it all over my glove."

He smiled.

"This is my baby," he said. "I have to take care of it."

And then there's infielder Darwin Barney.

"I am very particular about my glove," said Barney, who carries five gloves, the exact same make and model, on all road trips. "I never use my game glove except to play in the game. I don't use it during BP. I don't play catch with it before a game. The first time I touch it on the day of the game is when I'm running out to my position to start the game. If I play catch with it too often, it can make the pocket too deep. The other four gloves, I rank them. My number 2 glove is next in line. One year in Washington, I went to my backhand and the ball popped out of my glove. That was it for that glove. I threw it away—in the trash can—and never used it again. It lasted a year and a half, but that was it. I couldn't use it anymore." His number 2 glove became his game glove. "Each glove I have is at a different level of being broken in," he said. "My number 5 glove isn't ready to be a gamer, but it will be."

Marlins utility man Jeff Baker is nearly as particular about his many gloves. He has a glove to play second base, another to play third base, one for the outfield, and a mitt for first base.

"No one touches my glove for second base or my glove for third," he said. "They are different. My glove for second base is 11½ inches, my glove for third is 12 inches. At second, I need a smaller glove because I have to know when I reach into my glove to grip the ball, it has to be in the same place every time, it can't get lost in my glove. If someone puts my glove on his hand, and stretches out my glove, and now it's a quarter of an inch off, then we have problems. That may be the difference between making the double play or not. At third base, I need the extra half inch in the glove. The ball hit down the line, that half inch might be the difference between getting an out, or the ball going for a double. The ball hit to my left, that half inch might be the difference between a hit and a double play. Even on the ball hit right at me at third, mentally I feel better with that extra half inch."

Baker said he isn't as particular about his outfield glove or his first baseman's mitt. "I used to have [pitcher] Kerry Wood break in my first baseman's mitt because he loves to take throws at first base during BP, and he has really big hands, and I also don't have time to break in four different gloves during spring training," he said. "I used to have our video guy [Naoto Masamoto] break in my outfield glove because he loves to shag during BP. But I would never let either guy touch my other gloves. Kerry's big hands would ruin those gloves. But all my gloves, I'm working about a year behind on each. The four I will use this year, I had broken in last year. The gloves I'm breaking in this year, I'll use next year."

Reds second baseman Brandon Phillips carefully places five gloves in his locker. He has three practice gloves, all significantly smaller than his game glove; a smaller glove helps him "look" the ball into his glove a little better and a little longer. He has a backup game glove and his game glove, which was placed pocket-side down, with a batting glove strategically placed where his hand enters the glove. "You can touch my practice gloves, but no one touches my game glove, no one," Phillips said. "I put the batting glove on top of my glove so I'll know if someone has touched my glove. If the batting glove has moved, someone touched my glove. [Angels pitcher Mat Latos] held my glove once, but he didn't put it on. Defense is important to me. If he'd put his hand in my glove, we'd have fought."

And then there is ex-A's infield coach Mike Gallego, a career .239 hitter who played thirteen years in the major leagues because of his defense, which required the proper care of his glove.

"Earthquake Series," Gallego said of the A's–Giants World Series in 1989. "We [the A's] are in the clubhouse at 5 p.m. The earthquake hits, the lights go out, everything is dark. The place is shaking. Guys are running all over the clubhouse, trying to get out of there. I was halfway out when I realized that I had forgotten my glove! I ran back into the clubhouse—we didn't know if the place was going to collapse—and found my locker . . . in the dark. I got my glove. I couldn't leave my glove behind. That's my livelihood, my glove."

It is the best game because the players, at least some of them, are so human and so well-rounded. Mets right fielder Michael Cuddyer was the number 1 pick—ninth overall—of the Twins in 1997. Some kids don't go to school on the day of the June draft, they stay home to celebrate, but Cuddyer was taking a calculus test when his principal interrupted the class and escorted Cuddyer into the hall to inform him of the Twins' decision. The principal then made an announcement over the high school's public address system. Then Cuddyer went back to class *to finish the test*. When I asked if that story was all correct, Cuddyer said, "Yes, except it was a *pre*calculus test." And that's why the Twins would send all their young players to Michael Cuddyer and tell them, "Just be like him."

Cuddyer also is an accomplished magician. I have seen his act; it is phenomenal. "My first big-league camp, no one knew who I was. I went up to a bunch of veteran players, including Kirby Puckett, who were playing cards in the middle of the clubhouse," said Cuddyer. "I asked them, 'Do you want to see a card trick?' It was a good one. They couldn't believe it. After that, I was one of the guys." Not everyone loved his magic. "When [second baseman] Luis Castillo was with us, I did a card trick for him," Cuddyer said. "He's from right on the line between the Dominican and Haiti. He has some . . . I don't know, black gods thing going. He saw me do this trick and said, 'Whoo.' The next day, he moved his locker across the room. He didn't want to locker next to me anymore."

One of Cuddyer's ex-teammates in Colorado, pitcher Jeremy Guthrie, used to ride his bike to the ballpark every day in spring training. "He pitched in a game in Scottsdale, then got on his bike—still in full uniform, with his glove on the handlebars—and rode five miles back to our facility," Cuddyer said. "It was like a scene from *The Sandlot*."

Another of Cuddyer's former teammates, first baseman Doug

Mientkiewicz, missed a sign at Tiger Stadium, and was punished by then-Twins manager Tom Kelly. "I missed a hit-and-run," Mientkiewicz said. "After the game, I had to go back on the field, lead off of first base, look for the sign, take off running, and slide into third. I had to do it three times. There are 50,000 people in the stands, and I'm running the bases. The security guys thought I was some fan running on the field. I had to say, 'No, I'm a player. I missed a sign.'"

When outfielder Raúl Ibañez was in his early 20s, trying to make a big-league team, he went to the minor leagues to learn how to catch, thinking he could improve his value by becoming a team's third catcher. "The first game I ever caught, I completely missed the first pitch, a fastball. The ball hit the umpire right in his chest," Ibañez said. "He said, 'What the hell are you doing?' I said, 'Sorry, I've never caught before.'" Ibañez was never needed as a third catcher, but through his relentless work ethic, he was a World Series hero. He hit more than 250 home runs, more home runs than anyone else with the last name beginning with I, and joined Davey Lopes and Hank Sauer as the only players in history to hit more homers in their 40s than they did in their 20s. Think about that.

Infielder Craig Counsell played parts of sixteen years in the major leagues despite looking like a librarian, and with a batting stance that looked like a man stuck in a phone booth with a bee. But he persevered. In his last spring training, he smiled and said, "The other day, I got asked for my credentials at the security gate. I came into the park with Tom Haudricourt [a baseball writer], and the security guy thought I was a member of the media. When I first came up, they thought I was a bat boy. Now that I'm 39 years old, they think I'm a writer."

Dodgers pitcher Bronson Arroyo is an accomplished musician; he once played a set with Pearl Jam. "My life is complete,"

Arroyo said. "I have met Eddie Vedder and Ozzie Smith. I can die a happy man."

Giants third-base coach Tim Flannery also is a terrific musician and singer; before a World Series game in 2014, he sang, in uniform, the national anthem with two members of the Grateful Dead. "They came to me at the last minute and told me I was singing," Flannery said. "I told them, 'I would like a little time to practice.' The Dead said, 'No time. We're on. Sing.'"

Former major leaguer Conor Jackson is the son of an actor, and while at the University of California, Jackson majored in drama. "Everyone on our baseball team knew I was a drama major, but I never told anyone on the team when I would be performing in a play," he said. "If I did, and if the team showed up drunk, it would be a disaster. We did a bunch of little plays. If thirty guys showed up, that would be about half the audience. That wouldn't work. I would look around the curtain before the show, wonder, 'Do I know anyone out there?' But it was great. I loved it."

Angels pitcher C. J. Wilson says, "I just love everything. I'm the opposite of ADD, if there is such a thing." He has been on an African safari, done an oil painting, driven race cars, reviewed movies, and stayed celibate until he got married. He is also one of the greatest fans of the TV show *Lost*, and in great detail, he explained what the hell happened in that show, especially in the final episode. "They use an element of non-linearity," he said. "I'd have fifteen people over for a dinner party and we'd watch *Lost*. No one talked, no one texted. In the commercials, we would discuss it. I was drawn into that universe. When the show ended for good, it was like a relationship ending." He also explained the ending of the movie *Inception*, and in doing so, he used the word *ambiguous* and the phrase *spiritual zenith* in the same complete sentence. Wilson said of the movie *The Black Swan*, "The sound design in that film was incredible."

It is the best game because it can be so funny. In spring training 2011, the Twins signed an infielder from Japan named Tsuyoshi Nishioka. Several veteran players convinced Twins center fielder Denard Span to introduce himself to Nishioka, and welcome him to the team. So Span, ever classy and polite, approached the player he thought was Nishioka, but, as part of the prank, it was actually infielder Ray Chang. So Span went to Chang, bowed respectfully, introduced himself, then asked, "Do you speak any English?"

"Sure I do," Chang said, "I'm from Kansas City!"

The whole clubhouse howled, including Span.

The Mets clubhouse in spring training 2011 was a constant laugh because that spring, they organized a bowling league. "We have forty professional athletes, and thirty-eight of them stink at bowling," manager Terry Collins said, smiling. David Wright was the best bowler on the team; he rolled a 259 his first game. Reliever Jason Isringhausen was the second-best bowler on the team. "He is good at any sport that involves beer," Wright said. Catcher Josh Thole was on Isringhausen's team. "He bowled an 88 one game," Isringhausen said with a smile. Thole was then the primary catcher for the Mets, and they gave him unlimited grief about being somewhat cross-eyed, which he doesn't dispute, and he has fun with it. "He's the only guy I know that you can poke in both eyes with one finger," Wright said playfully. "When he bowls, he's not sure what lane he's going to bowl in because one eye is going in one direction and the other is going in the other direction."

It was in spring training 2011 that the new Brewers coaches had to stand in front of the team and introduce themselves and provide a career highlight. Jerry Narron explained his highlight was hitting a home run in the upper deck at Tiger Stadium. Then-Brewers first baseman Prince Fielder stood up and said, "I did that when I was 12!" Narron laughed, as did the whole team. Indeed. I saw Fielder hit home run after home run at the ballpark in Arlington at that age. He once told me he weighed 300 pounds when he was 12.

"We had an all-you-can-eat spaghetti night at my restaurant [in Arlington]," said former Rangers manager Bobby Valentine. "Prince, at 11, cleaned us out one night. We canceled the promotion."

It is the best game because it has a manager such as Joe Maddon of the Cubs. He is the Most Interesting Man in the World, an expert on rock and roll music, chocolate, wine, and everything in between. His Lafayette education serves him well every day. During a press conference at the 2008 World Series, he used the words *intuitive, intrinsic,* and *ameliorate* in complete sentences (I had to look up the last one). Twice, in two regular season games, I saw him arrive at the ballpark at 3 p.m. for a 7 p.m. game. He said, "If you think I have to sit in my office in my underwear drinking coffee at noon and going over the lineup to show everyone how hard I work at this, you have the wrong guy."

Maddon is all about making his players more relaxed and comfortable. He has routinely canceled batting practice—"rest is more important than repetition," he says—to help take their mind off that night's game. Once he brought a magician to the clubhouse a few hours before game time. "We had some guys hitting in the cage," Maddon said. "I went in there and told them, 'Stop hitting. You have to see this guy. He's great!'"

Maddon arranged for a local zookeeper to bring a 25-foot boa constrictor into the clubhouse. "The snake's name was Sadie. She ate every two weeks; one of her favorite things to eat were frozen rabbits," Maddon said. "I learned something that day. Some of our guys just left the room as soon as the snake was brought in. Some guys touched the snake, but nowhere near his mouth. And a couple of guys went right up near the head. I thought, 'Wow, maybe this is the type of guy I'm not going to worry about with two outs in the ninth.' We found that Sadie hadn't eaten in thirteen days, and when she started to poop on the floor, that's a sign that she's hungry. That's when we decided to get her out of the clubhouse."

Maddon also encourages his players to think independently, as he does. One spring, his first baseman, Carlos Peña, was thrown out on the bases during a drill. "He used the Martin Luther King freedom speech as his justification for being thrown out," Maddon said. "He said, 'Dr. King used to say that going to jail can be a good thing if you are going for the right reason.' Carlos made his case that getting thrown out at third base was not a bad thing if your reasoning was correct. My first baseman was quoting Dr. King. You have to love that."

And you have to love Giants manager Bruce Bochy, who is the best in the game, and is going to the Hall of Fame, and you would never know it from just talking to him. Bochy doesn't come across as a funny guy, but he is really funny, and I'm not just talking about his size 8¼ head, which has to be the biggest one in baseball. In the winter of 2011, Bochy tried skiing for the first time. "I thought I could do it; I'm still somewhat athletic. As it turns out, I'm not," he said with a smile. "I got on the ski lift, then I kind of slipped off, and the lift hit me in the back of the head. My gloves and skis and hat went flying; it looked like a yard sale. I didn't even try to ski after that. I went to the lodge and had a beer."

It is the best game because of players such as Derek Jeter. No matter what you hear about how good a guy he is, multiple it by five, and that's how good he is. I once asked one of Jeter's former teammates, Tino Martinez, to tell me something about Jeter that not everyone knows. "If he has one beer," Martinez said, "he is not getting behind the wheel of a car for any reason. Never." After the Yankees won the 2009 World Series, Jeter's fifth ring, my job was to do a postgame interview with him for ESPN TV. I followed him across the clubhouse, which was covered with champagne and screaming Yankees. Jeter dodged everyone and everything until he finally made it to a hallway outside the other side of the clubhouse. There were his mom and dad. He hugged them first, then he celebrated.

By my official rankings, Jeter retired as the third-best shortstop of all time, behind Honus Wagner and Arky Vaughan, a list I had written and had said on TV, more than once. During spring training 2014, his last spring training, Jeter approached me and said, "I need to talk to you about something." I was a little worried at first, but a few minutes later, he asked me respectfully, "Who is Arky Vaughan?" I explained that he played for the Pirates in the 1930s and '40s, a lifetime .318 hitter, and a great defensive shortstop. He thanked me and moved on. It occurred to me a short time later that he might have been asked about Vaughan, didn't know the answer, was embarrassed, and needed a working knowledge of him just in case he was ever asked again. With Jeter, it's all about being prepared.

It is the best game because of players like Corky Miller, who, if there was such a thing, would be the president of the Backup Catchers Club. It's a unique fraternity of guys who have been backup catchers their whole career. They bounce from team to team, from bullpen to bullpen, warming up pitchers, giving the starting catcher a rest, then warm up a few more pitchers. They are catching lifers; they play for a different team virtually every year, but they just don't play very much: Henry Blanco, Chris

Stewart, Chris Snyder, Koyie Hill, Brett Hayes, Yorvit Torrealba, and Gerald Laird, to name a few.

"I see Matt Treanor every spring," Miller said. "When you see one of us, you just kind of nod and smile at them. I looked at Matt, nodded, smiled, and said, 'Still grinding it out, huh?' He smiled back at me with that look of, 'Here we go again.'" Corky Miller played until nearly 40 years old. He made his major league debut in 2001, and he has played more than 200 games for the Reds, Twins, Red Sox, Braves, and White Sox. And yet he never played even 40 games in a season. He is the only non-pitcher in history to play that many games, without playing 40 in any season.

Corky Miller is the perfect name for a backup catcher. Baseball reference books list him as Abraham, and some teammates have called him that, but his real first name is actually Corky. His parents named him after a relative named Clark, who went by Corky. "My mom used to tell me if I ever became the president of the United States, I would go by C. Abraham Phillip Miller," Corky Miller said. "But I haven't come close to becoming the president."

It is the best game because of guys such as pitcher Ross Ohlendorf. He went to Princeton, he played for several major league teams, and he is the smartest person I've ever met in a major league uniform. Veteran major league pitcher Chris Young was a teammate of Ohlendorf at Princeton. "Oh, he is way smarter than I am," Young said when asked. "He is on a different level." Ohlendorf did not get an 800 in math on the SATs. "I got one wrong," he said, but took a similar test, and said without pretense, "I think I got them all right."

Princeton baseball coach Scott Bradley said, "There was a famous card game at Princeton when Ross played cards for the first time with his teammates. He raised in the middle of a hand. His teammates said, 'What in the world are you doing raising now?' Ross said, 'Three hands ago, Steve had an ace and a king . . .' He was able to recall plays from three previous hands. At that point, guys threw their cards down and said, 'Let's do something else.'"

At Princeton, Ohlendorf wrote his senior thesis on the Major League Baseball draft, examining, among other things, the investment and the financial return for the top players in the draft. "He is *so* smart," said then-Pirates shortstop Jack Wilson. "We give him a hard time about how smart he is, and he'll come right back at us. We'll say, 'Ross, what is the percentage chance of this or that happening?' And he'll say, 'The percentage chance of you winning that game of Pluck [a card game] is 65.678 percent, not 65.667 percent."

And they love him for his smarts. As Ohlendorf was explaining his thesis, then-Pirates closer Matt Capps walked by and said, "Is that the thesis that you stole from me?"

It is the best game because its history and tradition is like no other sport: only in baseball can the "modern era" be defined as 1900 on. And the players and events from one hundred years ago remain relevant today, which can't be said for football and basketball. The great players of the past are revered long after they have retired. Hall of Famer Paul Molitor, one of the game's classiest and most well-spoken guys, went to a banquet years ago. "Ted Williams was in the corner talking to Joe DiMaggio, and as soon as I walked in, Ted blows off Joe DiMaggio to come talk to me!" Molitor said. "I couldn't believe it. He started asking me questions like, 'What are you looking for on 2-0?' I was so intimidated. I didn't know what to say. Ted Williams is talking to *me*! I'm sure I sounded like a complete idiot."

Aaron Boone talks to everyone. He is a member of the only three-generation family of All-Stars: grandfather Ray; father Bob; Aaron, and brother Bret. At the 2014 All-Star Game in

Minnesota, Aaron Boone was in the same elevator as the great Hank Aaron. "I was too afraid to say hello," Boone said. "That is Hank Aaron!"

It is the best game because there is an art to keeping score. Many years ago, at the team's annual winter festival, Bob Di- Biasio, then the PR director of the Indians, would hold a seminar on how to keep score. After detailing an elaborate scoring play on the overhead projector, a nun—a nun!—from the back of the room raised her hand, interrupted, and said, "That's not how you score that play. Let me show you how *I'd* score that."

It is the best game because the best (and worst) movies are made about baseball. *Field of Dreams* will always be my favorite, but I loved *61*, the Billy Crystal movie detailing the Mantle-Maris home run chase in 1961. It was so authentic, so detailed, that when Crystal looked for someone to play the part of knuckleballer Hoyt Wilhelm in the movie, Crystal chose Tom Candiotti, a knuckle- ball pitcher that had just been released by the Angels. Crystal told him that he had to become Wilhelm and had to throw his best knuckleball.

"I had a blast. I had my own trailer. I got royalty checks; one was for sixty-one cents," Candiotti said. "So I threw Barry Pep- per [the actor playing Maris] about fifteen, seventeen knuckle- balls, and he never came close to hitting any of them. The catcher playing Gus Triandos couldn't catch the ball; I hit him in the mask several times. Poor Gus, I felt sorry for him. All we needed was a little dribbler up the first-base line, but Barry can't hit any- thing. So Billy comes out to the mound, he's laughing, and said, 'Tom, we have a problem. It's called "tape."' So I slowed down the knuckler, then one of them hits Barry right in the chest. The entire movie cast came running to home plate like I'd killed the star of the show. Barry is lying on the ground, he asked me, 'How hard was that one?' I said, 'That was 55 mph. You have to get up after that one.' So, he's all dirty now, he has to go get a new uniform and new makeup, and that takes about three hours. He comes back and still can't hit it. So Billy just rolled one up the line."

It is the best game because it raises so many unanswerable questions. Really, how can it be that the first complete games ever thrown by Dallas Braden and Philip Humber were perfect games? How can there have been two eighteen-inning games in postseason history, and both were started by Tim Hudson? How can Willie Mays, Hank Aaron, Barry Bonds, and Babe Ruth never have hit for the cycle, but Bengie Molina, the slowest player on earth, did? How could pitcher David Price, who is only 30 years old, name his dog Astro, claiming "I love *The Jetsons*." How can the Mets have once had Razor Shines as their third-base coach, a job that is to send people home, yet he played in 68 major league games, and never scored a run? How can Scott Sizemore play his first game ever at first base, and take part in a triple play, when Steve Garvey, Fred McGriff, Mark Grace, and Rafael Palmeiro played 8,599 games at the position combined, and never took part in a triple play? How can Drew Butera have caught two no-hitters in his career when Tony Peña caught 1,950 games without catching a no-hitter, the most games ever caught without catching a no-no? How can pitcher Madison Bumgarner hit more grand slams in a season (two) than Derek Jeter hit in his career (one)? And seriously, how can anyone not wear a protective cup when playing Major League Baseball? For Christmas presents one year, Cal Ripken Sr. gave his sons Cal Jr. and Billy metal protective cups, wrapped up, and told them to always wear them, and yet Astros third baseman Matt Dominguez does not, saying, "That's what my hands are for."

It is the best game because it is a hard game played by hard men. And there was no one harder than Pete Rose. You don't have to like him, you don't have to believe he should be in the Hall of Fame, but this story defines who he is, and who Major League Baseball players are. Rose served five months in a prison for tax evasion. He got out of jail at age 49. His son, Pete Jr., picked him up at the prison. Pete Sr. greeted his son, then asked a question.

"Where is the nearest batting cage?"

"Just down the street," Pete Jr. said.

Pete Sr. got to the cage and asked the proprietor which was the hardest-throwing machine. "The one over there is 85 mph," the man said. If you haven't seen 85 mph in a while, that's really fast. So Pete Rose got in the cage. By this time, a number of fans realized that the Hit King was in the cage, so they gathered around to watch. The first pitch came in. Pete Rose—age 49, just out of prison after five months—hit the first pitch right back at the pitching machine, a rocket up the middle on the first pitch at 85 mph. Rose looked at the crowd, threw the bat down, said, "Some fucking things never change!" and walked away.

2. THE HARDEST GAME

Sister Rose Never Faced Craig Kimbrel

JEFF CONINE, THE greatest player in Marlins history, was once asked a favor by a friend: despite little playing experience in baseball, this friend wanted to try to catch Robb Nen, who, at the time, was a great closer. He threw 100 mph with a slider that spun so fast it would cut your shirt and had a delivery that was beyond violent. Every spring training for years, I made it a point to stand as close as possible to a bullpen session by Nen so I could understand how terrifying it would be to face a major league pitcher throwing that hard.

"I think I can catch him," Conine's friend said.

"You can't," Conine said. "He would kill you."

So Conine told his friend that at the picnic they would be attending that day, Conine would throw to him, and if he could catch Conine, then he'd consider letting him catch Nen.

"The first pitch I threw was maybe 75 [mph] . . . I broke his watch," Conine said. "If not for his watch, I would have broken his wrist. He said, 'Okay, maybe I can't catch Robb Nen.'"

Maybe? To truly love and appreciate baseball at its highest level as I do, the most important acknowledgment is this: baseball is the hardest game to play. That is not to diminish in any way the breathtaking athleticism of NBA players, the insane courage of NFL players, the incredible toughness of NHL players, and the stunning skill of PGA Tour players. But baseball is parts of those games wrapped in one. It requires tremendous skill, and includes an underrated level of courage, toughness, and athleticism. When you watch a baseball game on TV, or even when you attend a game and sit in the upper deck, the game doesn't look particularly difficult to play from there. But the ball is rock hard, it travels at an incomprehensible velocity; you can't see, sense, or feel that unless you are on the field, where the sounds and speed would provide a new appreciation of the game's force.

"I went from managing in the dugout to being a first-base coach, and in doing so, I moved 100 feet closer to the field," said former Mariners manager Lloyd McClendon. "The first thing that struck me being that much closer was, 'God, the game is so fast.' And I played in the big leagues!"

And because so many people have played baseball on some level, even in Little League, some people think they actually understand what it's like to face Aroldis Chapman at 103 mph.

"My mom was watching a game on TV, and said to me the next day, 'How did you miss that 2-0 slider last night?'" said veteran infielder Mark Reynolds, who hit 224 home runs and struck out 1,398 times in his first eight seasons. "I had to say, 'Mom, it's not that easy.'"

Easy? A coach of a travel baseball team for 12-year-olds in Chicago grew tired of the parents yelling at their kids for striking out too much. So the coach, who pitched in the College World Series in the early 1980s, made the fathers of the players take batting practice against him.

Predictably, he embarrassed them, striking them all out, and two of them came to him and angrily asked, "Why did you do that to us?"

The coach said, "Because you have no idea how hard it is to play this game. So I humiliated you. And now you know."

Baseball is a hard game played by hard men, and what separates it from golf is the fear factor, which is real, whether it's a hitter facing a 95-mph fastball coming at his face, a pitcher that has just released the ball 53 feet from home plate, or the third baseman playing in on the grass with Gary Sheffield at the plate waving that bat menacingly.

"I love baseball, but I had fear," said Ahmad Rashad, a four-time Pro Bowl wide receiver. "I was never afraid playing football. I had equipment. I knew I was going to get hit. I was prepared."

Baseball is the ultimate skill sport, and it cannot be played well if a player is injured. With all due respect to football players, if a lineman breaks his hand, he can have it casted and wrapped, then hit someone with his head and be an effective player on Sunday. In baseball, a pitcher can have a huge blister on the middle finger of his pitching hand that prevents him from gripping the ball properly, and without that, he can't throw a pitch the way it needs to be thrown. Football players are so strong and so determined, but they have six days to heal before the next game. Baseball players almost always have a game the next day. Brian Jordan was a good outfielder for the Braves and Cardinals. He also played NFL football, but his baseball career ended because he was unable to stay healthy. What does that tell you? Ex-pitcher Rich Harden was a hockey player, a physical enforcer, but he couldn't stay healthy enough to play baseball.

"I can't believe how many games these guys play, and how well they play playing every day," said NBA great Magic Johnson after six months as a part owner of the Dodgers. "When we played a back-to-back in the NBA, it was a killer. These guys play a back-to-back every night. Last night, we [the Dodgers] played a night game on the East Coast, we flew across the country after the game, and we're playing tonight in L.A. I don't know how they do it."

Magic's sport is easier to play than baseball. It is easier to shoot a basketball than hit a baseball. The failure rate is much higher in baseball. A basketball player can have a terrible game, but goes home knowing that he made a couple of buckets, or a couple of good passes. But in baseball, "I can go a whole week and not feel like I did anything right," said former third baseman Buddy Bell. A great NBA jump shooter can miss seven shots in a row, but he *knows* that eighth shot is going in. A major league player can go three games without getting a hit and starts to wonder if he'll ever get another hit.

"When you're in a slump, you go to bed at night and you lie there and your mind is racing and you think about everything imaginable: your bat model . . . your bat size . . . your pitch selection . . . how you are wearing your pants," said Mets third baseman David Wright. "But when you're going good, you can sleep very well. But on the whole, I would say that most Major League Baseball players don't sleep well at night. The game is too hard."

Great NBA players don't go from scoring 25 points a game on 48 percent shooting one year to 6 points a game on 18 percent shooting the next, but the baseball equivalent happens all the time. Great NFL quarterbacks don't go four games into a season without a 100-yard passing game, or a touchdown pass, but in baseball, that happens. In baseball, players go from good to bad, or vice versa, quickly and without explanation. Outfielder Carl Crawford was a star for the Rays, signed a huge free agent deal with the Red Sox, and wasn't close to being the same player. "When he was with Tampa, we used to say, 'We hate him,'" one

Red Sox player said. "Then he joined our team and we said, 'We hate him.'"

The mental part of the game can be so stressful, a slump can become so overwhelming, the only way to ease a player's mind is to get two hits that night. In the late 1980s, former Oriole outfielder Brady Anderson was a passenger in a car driven by teammate Rene Gonzales, who was going far too fast on a very dangerous road late at night in the rain. Anderson said to Gonzales, "Gonz, if I wasn't hitting .178, I'd ask you to slow down."

On the final day of the 1984 season, after going 0 for 3 with three strikeouts in a perfect game thrown by the Angels' Mike Witt, Rangers outfielder George Wright, who finished the season in a terrible slump that left his average at .243, was asked what he was going to do next. He shook his head and said, "I'm going to change my name and move to Africa."

Adam Dunn had a pretty good run for ten years, averaging 35 home runs per season, and hit at least 40 in a season five years in a row. But in 2011, he dropped to 11 home runs, batted .159, and had 177 strikeouts—he and Mark Reynolds are the only players to qualify for a batting title and finish a season with a higher strikeout total than a batting average. Dunn offered no explanation for his epic struggles; he tried everything to get out of it, but nothing worked. Marlins manager Ozzie Guillen, who was Dunn's manager that year in Chicago, said, "I love Adam Dunn, he is my favorite player ever. He was the worst player I've ever seen that season. But after every game, he stood at his locker and took it."

The following year, Dunn recovered from his horrendous season, and had a pretty good year. I asked him for the strangest piece of advice he had received the season before. Dunn laughed out loud and said, "My wife, not a great baseball fan, asked me, 'Have you ever considered batting right-handed?'"

That wasn't so funny to Hall of Famer Mike Schmidt. "When I was really going bad, even in the prime of my career, if you had told me that I would have a better chance of hitting with my back to the pitcher, I would have tried it," Schmidt said. "You will listen to anyone. You will do anything to get out of a slump."

That's how hard it is. And yet, I am amazed how many people don't view it that way. I love stupid hypothetical sports questions, my favorite being: could a 58-year-old man that hasn't played since high school put a ball in play in a hundred at bats against a major league pitcher if that pitcher viewed it as a serious competition? The answer, of course, is *no*. Zero. No chance, no balls in play, no contact, no doubt. Given it is a competition, and someone has to win and lose, and the pitcher would lose if the 58-year-old put a ball in play, then the pitcher would not allow it. His first act would be to buzz the tower, that is, throw at the hitter's head, and that would be it for him; the fear of God would essentially end the competition. And yet, it's amazing how many people disagree, how many think they could put a ball in play. Tigers pitcher Justin Verlander is not a believer. I told him that I had a hypothetical question involving him. I didn't even get halfway through all of the elements of the question, and he said, "Zero!" I told him that I didn't finish the question, and he said, "I don't care! The answer is zero! The answer will always be zero!"

I posed the same question in 2014 on Twitter, using then-Braves closer Craig Kimbrel as the pitcher. Most people said "Zero!" but more than a few insisted that they could hit against Craig Kimbrel. Really?

Outfielder Matt Diaz was an opponent and a teammate of Kimbrel's. One spring, Diaz faced Kimbrel in batting practice. "Whoa," Diaz said, "I think I fouled off one pitch. His first pitch came in about thigh high and I thought, 'Hey, thanks, Craig, for grooving one.' But by the time the pitch got to the plate, the ball was up around my neck. The ball *does* rise no one matter what anyone tells you. Sister Rose was a great [high school] physics teacher and a really sweet lady, but she never faced Craig Kimbrel."

It's not just the difficulty of hitting that is unappreciated. A towering infield pop-up would be uncatchable for the average fan, let alone on a windy, sunny day. A hard-hit infield ground ball travels so quickly, the average fan would have virtually no chance to handle it cleanly, but big leaguers do it with their eyes closed. "I wasn't a good hitter," said a 45-year-old friend who does baseball on TV, but never played baseball in high school, "but I bet if you gave me a month to practice, I could play second base as well as an A-ball second baseman." Seriously? That A-ball second baseman was probably the best player ever to go to his high school, maybe the best player ever from his hometown. The TV guy/second baseman, with a month of workouts, couldn't throw out a runner at first on a routine ground ball three times out of ten. And he wouldn't make it through the month of workouts without getting hurt, or giving up.

Former Oriole Mike Devereaux was a terrific defensive outfielder, but he did not have a good throwing arm, at least by major league standards. A Baltimore radio talk-show host who wasn't athletic said on his show that *he* could throw better than Mike Devereaux. So Oriole outfielder Brady Anderson called him on it, made him come to Camden Yards, made him stand in shallow-to-medium right field before a game, and made him throw a baseball to home plate. Anderson brought Orioles shortstop Cal Ripken along for the experiment. Ripken would be stationed at the plate, but he did not bring his glove to retrieve the throw.

"Aren't you going to bring your glove?" Anderson said.

"I won't need a glove," Ripken said.

The talk-show host's throw never got near home plate; it died in the infield grass after a short roll.

"Don't you ever say again that you can throw better than a big leaguer!" Anderson yelled.

That was a talk-show host, but many world-class athletes from other sports have worked out with major league teams, or thrown out the first ball at a baseball game, and more often than not, the results were not good. Some were embarrassing. There aren't many more athletic point guards than the Wizards' John Wall, but his first ball toss at a Nationals game was pathetic. I was on the field at Tropicana Field when Darrelle Revis, the best cover corner in the NFL at the time, had to throw out the first ball at a Rays game. He looked at me and said, "How do I do this? I've never done this before." Not just thrown out a first ball, but he'd never thrown a baseball before. And it looked like it. His first pitch was awful.

I covered the Celebrity Softball Game at the All-Star Game in 2014 at Target Field. One of the celebrities was then-Vikings running back Adrian Peterson, who is an amazing athlete, but he threw a softball like . . . if I said a girl, it would be disrespectful to some girls. I'm told that LeBron James—for me, the best athlete in the world; no one else at 6'8", 265 pounds has ever run and moved like him—has taken batting practice with a major league team, and it was ugly. And one member of the San Francisco Giants told me that the worst athlete/entertainer that he has ever seen work out with the Giants was . . . Jerry Rice. The greatest receiver in the history of football, maybe one of the five greatest NFL players ever, couldn't get a ball out of the cage, couldn't throw, and couldn't catch a fly ball.

"I've told players from other sports," said Orioles center fielder Adam Jones, a great athlete, "that we [baseball players] could play their sport better than they could play our sport.'"

And that's the point, and that's the truth: baseball players are more well-rounded than the athletes from the other major sports. There are more two- and three-sport high school athletes playing in the major leagues than there are in the NBA, NFL, or NHL. (Former Expos/Nationals outfielder Brad Wilkerson was all-state in high school in *four* sports in Kentucky.) The intricate skills required to play baseball translate much better to other sports; baseball players are going to look more athletic playing any sport than the average football or basketball player. When then-49ers quarterback Alex Smith threw out the first ball at the Giants game, he didn't have a particularly athletic throwing motion, and he's a quarterback! But if we asked almost any baseball player to throw out the first football at an NFL game, it would look like he probably played quarterback in high school.

That's because many of them did. First baseman Joe Mauer was the top-ranked high school quarterback in America, and was headed to play at Florida State, when the Twins made him the number 1 pick in the June baseball draft. Veteran slugger Adam Dunn was a great high school quarterback that had a chance to play for the University of Texas, but chose baseball. Future Hall of Famer Todd Helton played quarterback at Tennessee, mostly behind Peyton Manning, but when Helton and other Rockies worked out with the Denver Broncos, Helton said, "You should've seen Matt Holliday throw. He looked like an NFL quarterback."

I am told that Albert Pujols can't throw a football, but we're guessing there wasn't much football in the Dominican Republic when he was a kid. "Yadier Molina is the greatest defensive player I've ever seen at any position. I've never seen a catcher throw like him—he can throw a strike to second with something on it from his knees—but he can't throw a football," Holliday said. "He threw one in the clubhouse. It went dead left and broke a TV."

Rays outfielder Grady Sizemore rushed for 3,108 yards his

senior year in high school. Hall of Famer Al Kaline told me he was a better basketball player in high school than a baseball player, and he won a batting title in the big leagues at age 20. Dodgers outfielder Carl Crawford was recruited to play football at Nebraska and basketball at UCLA, but chose baseball. Cubs center fielder Austin Jackson, Padres outfielder Matt Kemp, and, years before them, infielder Delino DeShields told me there was "no doubt" they could have played in the NBA if they hadn't chosen baseball. Reds center fielder Billy Hamilton, who scored 30 touchdowns his senior year as a receiver in high school, and averaged 28 points a game in hoops, told me, "Baseball is the hardest sport. Not even close. There are nights in baseball where it looks like I've never played the game before. That would never happen in the other sports. My athleticism would just take over."

Former Rangers outfielder George Wright, at age 23, was a great basketball player. I once asked him how many points a game he scored in high school, and he said, "I never played basketball until two years ago." Ex–first baseman Cecil Fielder looks too big and slow to play basketball, but he can dunk and he can play because, despite his girth, he is a great athlete. So is portly pitcher David Wells, who can dunk a basketball. Elliot Johnson, a journeyman infielder who doesn't look like much of an athlete, had a 44-inch vertical leap in high school. He put his best dunks on YouTube, but he caught so much heat from fans that he took it down.

In 1989, when I covered the Orioles, I asked all twenty-five players if they had ever dunked a basketball. I mean, even once, alone in an open gym; it didn't have to be in a game. Twenty-three of the twenty-five players told me that they had. I asked former outfielder Mike Cameron, who said he could dunk "any way you like," what percentage of big leaguers had dunked at least once.

"Seventy percent," he said.

Center fielder Cameron Maybin, who also can dunk any way you like, and is a cousin of former North Carolina hoops star Rashad McCants, said, "I'd say between 75 and 80 percent. I'll say 78 percent have dunked. I say that because on our team, we do a lot of other sports as a team, especially in spring training. Baseball players are great athletes. I asked [former Padres pitcher] Dustin Moseley [who is 6′4″] if he could dunk. He was offended that I asked. I thought it was a legit question. He said, 'Oh, I can dunk.'"

I asked future Hall of Fame pitcher Mike Mussina, in his baseball prime, this stupid hypothetical question: if Larry Bird, in his prime, were to shoot 100 free throws, not in game pressure or with game fatigue, and Greg Maddux, in his prime, were to throw 100 pitches in the bullpen, without game pressure or game fatigue, would Bird make more free throws out of 100, or would Maddux throw more strikes out of 100? Mussina, who was a great high school basketball player, said, accurately, "It wouldn't be close. Bird would win every time. It is easier to shoot a free throw than to throw a strike, if nothing more than the exertion needed to do each skill. I am sure that *right now*, I could make more free throws out of 100 than I could throw strikes out of 100. It's not even close."

The Orioles' J. J. Hardy is a Gold Glove shortstop. He can do almost anything he wants athletically, in part because his mom played on the LPGA tour and his father was a professional tennis player. Hardy has spectacular hand-eye coordination; he often catches ground balls with one hand.

"I wouldn't recommend it to kids, but it works for me," he said. Hardy is also the best Ping-Pong player on the Orioles, and perhaps in the big leagues.

Hardy has no match on the Orioles. "It does me no good to

play anymore," Hardy said. "If I win, I'm supposed to win. If I lose, it's a big story."

One day in spring training, pitcher Jason Hammel beat Hardy in Ping-Pong. Five minutes later, Hardy received a text from the Brewers' Ryan Braun, who was 2,500 miles away. It read: "I heard you lost in Ping-Pong."

"News travels fast when I lose in Ping-Pong," Hardy said.

Hardy acknowledges that he "wouldn't score two points" against professional Ping-Pong players because they practice every day. So do baseball players, raising their skill level to heights that few can appreciate. The only way to conquer the world's hardest game to play is to put in a relentless amount of time in the batting cage, on the mound, and in the field. And all the really good players, every one of them, work at their craft all the time.

Greg Maddux is a top-five pitcher of all time; he might be the greatest control pitcher in the history of the game and he is the smartest pitcher of his or any generation. Here's how good he is: for a three-year period, not one passed ball occurred with him on the mound. Not once in three years did the catcher set up down and away, and Maddux missed location up and in, and the catcher mishandled the pitch. Not once in three years did Maddux cross up his catcher and throw a pitch that he couldn't handle. By comparison, the anti-Maddux, Daniel Cabrera, had seven passed balls with him on the mound in one season.

Maddux's control was so good that with 999 walks and four starts left before he retired, "He told me there was no way he was going to walk 1,000 batters in his career," said ex-teammate Derek Lowe. "So he didn't walk anyone in his last four starts. Amazing."

Maddux always worked in between starts. "Sometimes, in a bullpen session, every pitch he would throw would be a fastball down and away because he knew that was his most important pitch," said Leo Mazzone, one of Maddux's former pitching coaches. "He was a genius. He would come in after seven innings and say, 'How many pitches have I thrown?' I'd say, '81.' And he'd say '82, you missed one.' He's the best that I've ever seen."

Ken Griffey Jr. will be the first number 1 pick in the country to make it to the Hall of Fame. When he signed, he and the other Mariner draft picks that year were invited to work out at the Kingdome to understand that that would someday be their final destination. Most 18-year-olds would be nervous hitting in a big-league park in front of big leaguers, but Griffey was so talented, he was hitting line drives all over the field as he was carrying on a conversation with members of the media. He took a rest after one round of line drives, then spent the next round blasting balls into the upper deck in right field. The Nationals' Bryce Harper, another number 1 pick in the country, did the same thing the day he officially signed. After showing everyone how he could use the whole field, he hit the last pitch of the round into the third deck at Nationals Park, as if to say, "I can do that whenever I want."

Pirates center fielder Andrew McCutchen won the NL MVP in 2013, and finished third in 2014. When he was in the eighth grade, he went out for the high school baseball team and headed over to the field where the JV team was trying out. The varsity coach told him, "Son, you are with us." McCutchen won the county batting title that season as an eighth-grader.

Veteran outfielder Matt Diaz is from McCutchen's hometown in Florida. When Diaz was a Class AA player in the Braves system, he worked with McCutchen. "I worked with him three times and his hands were faster than mine, and I told him, 'That's all you need, you're a better hitter than I am right now,'" Diaz said. "He was 13 years old."

Dodgers ace Clayton Kershaw, at 26, had numbers—wins,

ERA, strikeout rate—that no pitcher in baseball history had ever matched at that age. Ever.

"His bullpens are like art," said former Dodgers manager Don Mattingly. "They are so regimented, so disciplined, so precise. Our young pitchers go watch his bullpen sessions. Most of them are older than Clayton."

The Angels' Mike Trout is a physical freak of nature. He weighs 235 pounds and runs like the wind. He is Mickey Mantle come back to life, yet his numbers his first three seasons are even better than the Mick's: Trout is the first player ever to finish in the top two of the MVP voting in each of his first two full seasons, and Trout did it in each of his first three seasons.

The Tigers' Miguel Cabrera won back-to-back MVP in 2012–13, keeping Trout from winning three MVPs in a row. Cabrera hit a walkoff home run in his first major league game, and he and Ty Cobb are the only players to hit cleanup in a World Series game at age 20.

"I've seen him, just messing around in batting practice, hit a home run down the left-field line, then the next pitch, go to left-center, then to dead center, then to right-center, then the right-field line," said former Tigers manager Jim Leyland. "I've never seen anything like it."

When Cabrera was dismantling the Orioles during one series in 2014, Baltimore manager Buck Showalter told his team in the dugout during the game, "I hope you guys appreciate what you're watching here; that's one of the ten greatest hitters of all time."

The best hitter I've ever seen is Barry Bonds. So, just for a second, forget about steroids, which I know is impossible. "I played with the Giants for one year [2004], and I've never seen anything like Barry, nothing even close," said veteran catcher A. J. Pierzynski. "The first series of the season, we were in Houston. He announced to the team, 'I'm not going to hit any homers in this series because I want to tie Willie [Mays, his godfather, on the all-time home run list with 660] when I get back home [to AT&T Park]. I'm going to get a bunch of hits here, but no homers.' So he went like 4 for 9 with three walks that first series, but no homers. So we go home, and he tells us, 'Willie is here today, so I'm going to hit a home run today.' And then he did. The next day, he told us, 'Willie is here again today, I'm going to hit another one today.' And then he did. I had never seen anything like it."

Most of the best players, such as Bonds, were predisposed to play baseball. It was in their genetic profile. It is what they planned to do from a young age. That was not the case with Royals center fielder Lorenzo Cain. He's a great athlete, big, fast, and strong, but he didn't even pick up a baseball until he was a sophomore in high school, when the baseball coach asked him to try out for the team.

"They gave me a glove for a left-handed thrower, so I threw left-handed," Cain said. "After a few minutes, I said, 'I think I throw better with this hand.' I was so raw. I am still so raw. It takes so long to learn this game. It is so hard."

Cain made it because of his great athleticism and work ethic. Mike Gallego, a former infield coach with the A's, made it thirteen years in the big leagues through sheer will. No one worked harder. "I couldn't hit [.239 lifetime], so in order to stay in the big leagues, I had to be the best defensive player I could be," he said. "I used to count every bounce on every ground ball hit to me: one, two, three, four, five, whatever. That made me look the ball into my glove."

That kind of dedication cannot be measured. Yet given how impossibly difficult the game is to play, we are constantly trying to determine a new way, a better way, to evaluate the players; hence the sabermetric revolution we are in, and likely will stay in, for many years to come. I love what we are trying to do. I love that organizations have hired teams of statisticians that can, in some cases, determine a better way to make out a lineup, a better way to decide the best player to draft, and a better way to determine if that free agent player is worth $100 million over five years. I love that the Astros hired a rocket scientist from NASA to help in the evaluation of players. I love data. The more data we have, the better. That is indisputable. And major league teams have more data now than ever.

But it is crucial to keep the human element as part of the equation, given that baseball is the most human of all the major sports, and given its degree of difficulty, its failure rate, its mental aspect, and its ceaselessly long season. No one loves the numbers more than I do, but numbers don't measure everything, especially when it comes to evaluating defense. And in the end, I am going to trust Buck Showalter's eyes more than a set of statistics devised by someone who never played the game. Years ago, the front-office guys for the Rangers asked Showalter to play Nelson Cruz, a corner outfielder, in center field because the advanced metrics suggested he could play center field. Showalter assured them that Cruz couldn't play center field, but he'd try it. His team wasn't going to the playoffs, and it was a good time to experiment. It was supposed to last two weeks. After one week, the front-office guys called it off, acknowledging that Showalter was right: Cruz couldn't play center. One of the young guys didn't mean to insult Showalter, but he did, by asking him, "How did you know?" Showalter knew because he was a good player in his day, he has worn a uniform for forty years, he recognizes first-step quickness, he knows what a good jump is. All those years in uniform, as a player, and as a manager; that's how he knew.

Sabermetics can't measure what is going on inside a player's head when he is standing in the outfield, with so much time to think about his 0 for 20, and wondering what's going to happen to his children once the bitter divorce with his wife is finalized. It cannot measure what a player goes through mentally when he's trying to hit a 95-mph fastball the day after burying his beloved father. Sabermetrics can't measure heart. Daniel Boone pitched in the big leagues at 140 pounds, re-creating his career as a knuckleball pitcher. He is a direct descendent of *the* Daniel Boone, a folk hero, a war hero. When asked to confirm how brave Daniel Boone must have been, Daniel the pitcher said with respect: "But I bet he didn't have the courage to throw a knuckleball on 3-2 with the bases loaded."

Sabermetics can't measure the innate feel for the game that some players have, such as Cal Ripken, and that other players don't. The Yankees drafted left-handed pitcher Brien Taylor with the number 1 pick in the country in 1991, thinking they would have a dominant pitcher for fifteen years. When he was asked in his first spring training to do what is known as the "inside move"—an easy maneuver in which the pitcher picks up his front leg and pivots toward second base for a pickoff throw—he picked up the wrong leg. He had never made that move before. He never pitched in the big leagues because he got hurt in a bar fight, but also because he didn't understand the subtleties of the game, one former instructor said, he didn't work enough, and he wasn't a good enough athlete to make the necessary adjustments.

Sabermetrics can't measure the wet spot in shallow right field at Fenway Park, which, if you don't know it's there, can cause a right fielder to lose the grip on the ball when he charges a single and comes up throwing. It cannot measure the height of the mound at old Veterans Stadium in Philadelphia and at Dodger Stadium—the mounds were clearly higher than the mounds in other ballparks.

"The first time I pitched in L.A., in the '66 World Series," said former Orioles pitcher Jim Palmer, "I almost fell off the back of the mound. It was that steep."

Sabermetrics can't measure that horrible piece of turf at the Rogers Centre in Toronto: when a ball hits that patch at the precise angle, the ball will bounce dead right.

Sabermetrics can't measure the speed of an infield surface. "Wow," said Giants shortstop Brandon Crawford at the batting cage before Game 3 of the 2014 World Series in Kansas City. "I've never played here. This infield here is way faster than at our park."

Sabermetrics can't measure the nuances of right field at San Francisco's AT&T Park. Former Giants outfielder Nate Schierholtz said there are nineteen different surfaces—fence, brick, metal, etc.—that a batted ball might hit, and whatever surface the ball hits will determine where and how far the ball will carom.

Sabermetrics can't measure the impact that a brilliant defensive catcher such as the Cardinals' Yadier Molina has on his pitching staff, the faith he brings to his pitchers that the sign he puts down is going to be the right pitch to throw. Molina runs the pitching meetings. When a pitcher once suggested in a meeting that they throw a certain hitter a slider on 2-0, Molina said, "No, we did that with him three years ago. He hit it out of the ballpark."

Sabermetrics cannot measure the confidence that a Royals pitcher had in 2014 when he looked around and saw Alex Gordon, Jarrod Dyson, and Lorenzo Cain in the outfield. "With those guys," said pitcher James Shields, "if it's in the air, it's caught. Knowing that changes everything. You pitch differently, and better, knowing they are out there."

Sabermetrics can't measure how the pressure on a young player can affect him. "I made an error behind Gaylord Perry when he was a veteran pitcher and I was just a kid," said Giants broadcaster Duane Kuiper, then with the Indians. "He turned and screamed at me, 'If you ever make another error behind me, you'll never play another inning on this team!' I was scared to death."

Sabermetrics can't measure instinct. "And Billy Hamilton has the best instincts on the bases that I've ever seen," said Reds veteran coach Billy Hatcher. "He has never even seen a pitcher before, and gets a huge lead against him, knowing he can always get back."

Sabermetrics can't measure what happens when a team knows the opposing pitcher is tipping his pitches: no one was better than Roberto Alomar at watching a pitcher, and finding the subtlest move that alerted him that an off-speed pitch, not a fastball, was coming.

Sabermetrics can't measure a player's pain tolerance. Ex-Brewer Dan Plesac said Hall of Famer Robin Yount "played—and played well—on days when he couldn't even walk."

But these days, we've stopped talking to the players about the wet spots at Fenway and the fast infield in KC, and we've essentially stopped watching the games. We're making too many determinations on a player's value, or who the MVP should be, based on a set of statistics on our computer screens rather than what we seen on the field with our eyes. Late in the 2013 season, then-Reds manager Dusty Baker attended an organizational meeting—a baseball meeting—to determine the direction of the team. The first person asked to offer an evaluation was the sabermetric guy in the corner, the guy that had never played, as opposed to the manager of the team, the guy that played nineteen years in the big leagues and had worn a major league uniform for forty-five years. That's just not right, but it's one reason that Baker was fired by the Reds—because he did not embrace the sabermetric revolution.

It is a concept with great value, and it should be heard. To not look at the data is foolish, but to look at the data as having all the answers is even more foolish. It is a collision of new-school statistics and statisticians against old-school managers, coaches, and instructors. Neither side is right, neither is wrong; there is so much to be gained from listening to both sides.

"I listen," said Pirates manager Clint Hurdle, who is as old school as it gets, "because some of these numbers don't lie. Look at all the shifting we do today. We shift because the numbers show that this guy is going to hit the majority of the balls he puts in play over here, so we're going to play our guys over here. It only makes sense. Back when I played [1977–87], when you hit a hard ground ball up the middle, it was a base hit. Not anymore."

So much in the game has changed since Hurdle first played in the big leagues. But this will never change: no matter how we choose to evaluate it, baseball will always be the hardest game to play. And sometimes it takes a Magic Johnson, a world-class athlete, a Hall of Famer in another sport, to really concentrate on baseball for the first time, and be stunned by its degree of difficulty.

"Matt Kemp says he can beat you in one-on-one," I said to Magic.

Magic was 51 at the time. Kemp was 28 when he made his bold prediction.

"Look," Magic said with a huge smile, "that's *my* sport. Baseball is his sport. He can't beat me in *my* sport. No way. Just like I would never say I could beat him at his sport. No way. I don't want to play his sport. His sport is way too hard."

3. HIT BY PITCH

It Still Hurts Today. He Hit Me in 1997.

IT IS WHAT chases kids from baseball at an early age, terrifies parents, and eventually keeps good players from being great: that shiny new 5-ounce baseball, which we like to refer to as a pearl, hitting a body part at a high rate of speed. When you are hit by a pitch, the elegance and romance of that pearl is replaced by piercing, pulsating, primal pain. It is pain that can last for weeks, that can leave a hideous mark that can last for months, and that can instill a fear that can last forever. It is pain that the average fan would experience once, then never go near home plate again. It is pain that major league players experience monthly, weekly, even daily, yet they keep getting back in that batter's box with a courage that deserves our complete admiration. It is what separates them from the rest of us.

"To me, the hit-by-pitch epitomizes the game of baseball," said veteran catcher John Baker. "The hit batsman, and the game, is all about, 'How much can you handle? How much pain can you handle? How much failure can you handle? How much embarrassment and fear can you handle?' Those that handle it best are the ones that play the game for a long time."

And yet, hit-by-pitch numbers are confusing. Former Braves infielder Mark Lemke holds the major league record for most plate appearances—3,664—without getting hit by a pitch, yet Lemke got hit by a pitch plenty of times in the minor leagues. ESPN's John Kruk got hit by a pitch twice in 4,603 plate appearances. He explained that if he stood way off the plate, he could take the ball on the inside part of the plate and either pull it or hit it the other way, so pitchers rarely tried to pitch him inside. Mickey Mantle was hit 13 times in part because he was a switch-hitter. Tony Gwynn was hit only 24 times in part because his eyes and his pitch recognition were so good, he could get out of the way in time.

The all-time leader in being hit by a pitch is Hughie Jennings, whose career began in the 1800s. He was hit 287 times, once every 19.3 plate appearances. Craig Biggio was hit 285 times, followed by Tommy Tucker (272), Don Baylor (267), Jason Kendall (254), and Ron Hunt (243). Baylor, big and burly and tough, was once asked which one of the 267 hurt the most, and he grunted and said, "None of them." Kendall, who isn't as big or burly, but is as tough as they come, and got hit by pitches on purpose all the time, said of his 254, "They all hurt."

Former Expo/Giant F. P. Santangelo laughed and said, "I'm in the hit-by-pitch Hall of Fame: most hit-by-pitches in a season by a switch-hitter: 25. I was a .245 hitter. I hit leadoff. I had to get on base any way I could. On-base percentage was my only good statistic. I learned how to lean in and get hit by strikes. Kendall and I had a side bet one year on who could get hit most. We bet a case of beer. I'd see him on the field before a game and I'd say, 'I'm at 17,' and he'd say, 'I'm at 18.' I think I still owe him a case of beer."

> *When that ball is coming at your head at 95 mph, that is*
> *the fear of God. That sound you hear is the thumping of*
> *your heart.*
>
> —Mike Macfarlane, former major league catcher

It is not an exaggeration: the fear of God, the thumping of your heart. At that moment, when the ball is traveling at an incomprehensible rate of speed, the hitter has to make a decision. "And you have .28 seconds to figure it out," said veteran outfielder Nick Swisher.

Former major leaguer Bobby Valentine, whose cheekbone was shoved dangerously close to his brain after being hit by a pitch in the face more than forty years ago, said, "For all humanoids, those who breathe, when someone throws a baseball from 60 feet, and throws it really hard, the first thought is always, always, always, 'Do I duck or swing?' The difference is the time that people take to decide whether to duck or to swing."

The average person ducks when the ball is coming near him, the big leaguer stays in and swings.

"The fans have no idea," said infielder Will Rhymes. "They don't realize that they wouldn't even stand in there and track a pitch against a major league pitcher. And they are smart not to stand in there. At least we know how we're supposed to get out of the way."

And yet sometimes, there is no chance of escaping a pitch that is headed right at you.

"You can tell, on some pitches, right out of the hand, that it's going to hit you, no matter what you do," said veteran outfielder Torii Hunter. "You can tell when it slips off the inside of his hand, and you're thinking, 'Oh, shit.' If it's coming at your head, you turn your head because you don't want it to hit you in the face because I'm too pretty to be hit in the face. So you turn so it will hit you in the back of the head. If it's coming at your ribs, you turn so it will hit you in the back of the bicep. If it's going to hit you in the knee, you turn so it hits you in the back of the leg. It's amazing how quickly the human body can move when you're trying to avoid something hitting you. You have to know your soft spots."

And even the soft spots hurt.

"It's a helpless feeling up there," said journeyman outfielder Brennan Boesch, "when you know you can't get out of the way. At that point, you just pray it doesn't hit you in the face."

And yet, there is no time for prayer.

"There are two types of thoughts when the ball leaves the pitcher's hand," said veteran outfielder Shelley Duncan. "The first one, you see the ball, and about halfway to the plate, you have that 'Oh, shit!' moment. If you don't get ready for it, that's when you get hurt. The other one is the pitch that you know right away, you are going to wear it. You can turn your body, you get ready to get hit, but it all happens so fast. You have to make the adjustment because one second you are calm, then a split second later, your heart is racing."

Catchers have been known to yell, "Watch out!" when a pitch is headed for a hitter; the Blue Jays' Russell Martin has done that more than a few times. Ex-Braves outfielder Matt Diaz said, "I've yelled, 'Oh!' when the pitch was headed at me because I was sure it was going to hit me, then it didn't. I turned to the catcher, and he was laughing his ass off. The umpire was chuckling. I said, 'I thought it was going to hit me.' They said, 'We did, too.'"

Orioles center fielder Adam Jones said, "Sometimes, you just know it's going to hit you as soon as it leaves his hand, and you think, 'Oh, shit.' It freezes you up. You brace for impact."

*It was like my face was crushed by a bowling ball, a bowl-
ing ball going 95 mph.*
     —Braves hitting coach Kevin Seitzer, on being hit in
              the face by a pitch by Scott Erickson in 1995

Some major league players can't remember anything about a walk-
off home run that they hit, or a game-turning grand slam, but
ask any player about the hardest he has ever been hit by a pitch,
and he will have the answer, without hesitation, with complete
detail, always including the velocity. The pain at that moment of
impact is unfathomable, and unforgettable.

"Danys Baez hit me with 97 [mph] in the ribs in 2002,"
Hunter said. "I lost my breath. I was gasping for air. It hurt so
much. The ball just dropped at my feet. Those are the ones that
hurt the most, the ones that hit you and drop straight down. And
what did I do after I got hit? I just picked the ball up and threw
it back at him. At that point, it just hurt so much, I was seeing
red. I couldn't think straight anymore. It hurt so much, I couldn't
think."

That was Robin Ventura's hilarious excuse for famously charging the mound after being hit by Nolan Ryan, who got Ventura
in a headlock and started pounding away. "He threw so hard, it
hurt so much, I didn't know what I was doing, so I just took off
after him because of the pain," Ventura said. "I got about halfway to the mound, came to my senses, and said, 'What am I
doing charging Nolan Ryan?' But I couldn't turn back then."

Diaz smiled and said, "I believe there is a connection that runs
directly from your ribs to your brain. I got hit in the ribs; it was
the worst. I kind of blacked out. When I woke up, I was yelling
at [Marlins catcher] Ronny Paulino. Not smart. He's like four
feet taller than me."

Mets third baseman David Wright said a shot to the ribs "will take your breath away. It's like jumping into freezing cold water. You need to take a knee to catch your breath. It hurts."

Swisher said, "I got hit by [Vicente] Padilla in the ribs at 97 [mph]. I was so angry, I just charged the mound because he had thrown at me twice before. I couldn't feel the pain because I was so angry. Man, that fucking hurts. The average fan has no idea how much that ball hurts. I am amazed. I see screaming line drives go in the stands, and fans try to catch it barehanded. They are crazy. I wouldn't try to catch that ball *with a glove on*. But nothing is worse than one in the ribs. My bruise there lasted a good three weeks."

Veteran infielder Mark Reynolds said, "The ribs are the worst. It's like getting hit with an uppercut, but without boxing gloves on. It knocks the wind out of you. When you see the guy bending over at home plate, he is catching his breath. He's taking inventory to make sure everything is still there. When the guy strolls to first, he's not Cadillac-ing it, he needs ten to fifteen [seconds] to catch his breath, and try to forget the pain. It is intense for thirty or forty-five seconds."

Hitters say that getting hit in the butt is the best place because it is flesh, not bone, and that getting one in the back doesn't hurt as much as a lot of areas. Hunter disagreed, saying, "Getting hit in the back really hurts, too. I tell people, 'Take your shirt off and let me hit you in the middle of your back with my open hand as hard as I can, and see how much that hurts.' With a baseball, multiply that by two . . . or three . . . and that's what it feels like. When you get hit like that, it's going to leave a mark, but as black as I am, it's not going to leave a mark for long, only a couple of days. But it hurts for a lot longer than that."

What about the back? "I was in Double-A, and [teammate] Melky Cabrera hit a home run, and he pimped it all around the

bases, and I thought, 'Oh, no, I'm going to get killed here,'"
Duncan said. "So Matt Lindstrom hit me in the back at 100
mph. When it hits you right, it's like someone slaps you in the
face. It wakes you up. The pain eventually went away, but whenever someone touched me on that place where I was hit, it would
hurt, and that lasted for at least a couple of weeks. The bruise
starts out black-and-blue, it looks like the eclipse of the sun, the
area around the mark left by the ball. Then it gets really blue. It
is pretty neat-looking."

Jones laughed and said, "That blue is just beautiful. It is so awesome what blood can do."

Hunter said hitters try to get hit in a soft spot. The knee is not
a soft spot.

"Kevin Brown hit me in the kneecap, broke my kneecap, and I
played with a broken kneecap for two months because I wasn't
coming out of the lineup," Santangelo said. "Earlier in the game,
I leaned in and took one off the thigh on purpose, and Kevin was
so mad, he said, 'So, you want to get hit?' and he hit me in the
kneecap with mid-90s [mph]. Years later, he gave me a bat with a
bull's-eye on it and he signed it, 'To F.P., my favorite target.' I
had to have surgery on that knee. It still hurts today . . . all the
time. He hit me in 1997."

"I got hit with a 97-mph fastball from Brandon League. It hit
me on the top of the knee; if it had hit me lower, it would have
shattered my kneecap," Baker said. "I take playing in the major
leagues seriously. You'd have to kill me to get me out of a game.
It happened in the seventh inning. I figured I would only have to
catch one more inning. I could do that. The bigger problem was
that it came two days after I got hit in the side of the head—that
required six stitches—after being hit with the backlash of Albert
Pujols's bat while I was catching. When League hit me, it really
hurt; my leg went numb, but as I was jogging to first, the cut on

my head opened up. I had blood running down the side of my face. So even though my knee hurt, it wasn't as bad as two days earlier. There is a scale of pain, a scale of feeling. Anything below the highest level doesn't hurt nearly as much as it should."

Ex-Cub' Eric Hinske said, "Sidney Ponson hit me on the inside of the knee with 95 [mph]. I thought I had been shot with a gun. I went down like a sack of potatoes. But I stayed in the game. You wrap it up and keep playing. The lump on my shin was there at least a month."

White Sox first baseman Adam LaRoche has been hit many times in his career, but none harder than the time he was hit in the back of the knee by a 90-plus-mph cutter by Josh Johnson.

"That's the worst pain I've ever felt on a baseball field," La-Roche said. "The ball hit me so hard, it bounced halfway back to the pitcher's mound. I went straight to the ground after that one. When I got back up, I had to take a knee. I was just trying not to throw up."

Rhymes fainted after being hit in the right forearm by a slider by Franklin Morales in 2012.

"It all happened so fast," Rhymes said. "I was looking for a fastball in. He threw a slider. You have to stay in there, you have to stand your ground. As soon as he let it go, I knew it was going to hit me, there was nothing I could do about it. When it hit me, I was stunned, but I thought, 'At least it didn't hit me in the head.' I thought, 'I broke my arm, but I'm glad it didn't kill me.' It was the first time I'd been hit on that bone. My arm felt dead, it went numb. There was tremendous pain, but I knew there was no one else to run for me. So I stayed in the game. I could run, but I knew I couldn't throw. When I got to first, I was angry because I knew my season was over. I was hitting .290. I was playing a lot.

"Then I started getting nauseous. I turned to Cuz (first-base coach George Hendrick) and said, 'I think I'm going to pass out.' Before I even finished saying that, I had passed out. While I was out, I had a dream. I can't remember what it was about. When I came to, I was looking at the ceiling of the Trop. It was a really weird effect, looking up at the ceiling. I came out of the game; my arm was hugely swollen, but it didn't get all black-and-blue. It took about ten days before it felt normal again, but I played two days later. I've been hit by 95 mph before, but not quite like that, in that spot. It is still tender to the touch."

Two months later, it was still tender. It is like that when 95 mph hits the bone.

Reynolds said, "I'd rather get hit in the head than in the wrist or the fingers or the hands. That can cost you a season."

Adam Jones said, "[Toronto's] Brandon Morrow hit me with 96 [mph] on the wrist, and here it is at least a month later, and it still hurts when I do anything with it. But it's one of the things you have to do when you are a big leaguer. I ice it, but it doesn't help. The only way to get it better is to rest it, but it's June 27. There is no time for rest. This is Major League Baseball. It is a minor inconvenience. Deal with it."

Former major leaguer Aaron Boone, now an ESPN analyst, was hit eighty times in his career. "Jamey Wright hit me right on the thumb in the same year that I broke my hand and got hit on the wrist," Boone said. "It was September. I got to first base, looked at the first-base coach, and said, 'Well, I just broke my thumb.' After the game, and for the next twenty-four hours, the pain was unbearable. They put a pin in my thumb. The next season, I got off to a really bad start because I could not grip the bat. For the first month of that season, I couldn't take a swing in the on-deck circle without pain because my thumb still hurt from September."

Swisher said, "I got hit in the back of the elbow by Jered Weaver. My fingers were locked in a fist for five minutes."

Santangelo said, "I got hit in the elbow, and for four pitches, as I was leading off first base, my hand was locked like a claw, I couldn't unclench my fist."

But getting hit in the head is something different—it can kill you. Seitzer got hit in the head in 1989 by Jack Morris. "I was afraid to open my eyes because I thought I was dead," Seitzer said. "When I finally did, I saw Mike Stanley's shin guards. I knew I was alive."

In 1994, Seitzer was hit in the right cheekbone by Melido Perez, but played the next day—the next day!—even though doctors warned him if he got hit in the same place, "My eyeball would drop into my cheek." Seitzer wore a protective bar on his helmet, but he took it off in 1995, then got hit by Erickson in the face. "That one hurt 10,000 times more than the first one," Seitzer said. He wore that protective bar until he retired two years later, and felt the need to say, "The only people in the world who could give me a hard time about wearing that are guys who were hit in the face twice—no one else."

Tony Conigliaro was hit in the face by Jack Hamilton in 1967. Conigliaro made a remarkable comeback to hit 36 home runs in 1970, but he was never the same because his vision was affected. Neither was Astros shortstop Dickie Thon after he got hit in the head by Mike Torrez in 1984, mostly because he couldn't see, either. Biggio got hit in the head by the Cubs' Geremi González in 1997. "I felt like I got hit in the head with a hammer," Biggio said. "My wife and our kids, and their class from school, were sitting upstairs in the luxury box. She was screaming, 'Please get up.'"

And he did. All big leaguers do. The rest of us don't.

"I got hit in the head twice," Reynolds said. "The first was by Collin Balester, mid-90s [mph] in Arizona; the roof was closed. They had to help me off the field that night. I had a concussion. There was a ringing in my ear. When I was lying on the ground, I looked up, and it was like the roof was right on top of me. It kind of freaked me out until I could get my vision back. It was a little blurry. It was a little scary. But I only missed a couple of games."

David Wright got hit in the head by a 93-mph fastball by Matt Cain in 2009.

"I remember the sound—it was just like a thud; that's a terrible sound," he said. "Obviously, it hurt a lot. I got headaches for a week. But you have to get back on that horse."

Kendall was once hit in the head by Danny Graves. "It was scary, but it hit me in the helmet, all helmet," he said. "It felt like I got coldcocked, like I just got punched in the jaw. But once you get your bearings . . . if you know where you are, then you are all right."

> *Never let them think they hurt you. Never. Just get your ass down to first base.*
>
> —Jason Kendall

Baseball is a hard game played by hard men. It has always been that way. It always will be.

"You do not show pain, that's the maxim, that's the code that ties in the locker room," John Baker said. "This is not soccer. There is no yellow card that comes out. You don't lie on the ground for twenty minutes, then hop up and start running again. You have to have respect for the game, for the guys that came before you. You have to show respect to the guys that faced Bob Gibson without wearing a helmet. I am wearing an arm guard at the plate, and a helmet that can take a 100-mph impact of a fastball. Ty Cobb didn't wear that helmet or those pads. Ty Cobb didn't rub it. There is a code of masculinity that exists in this game."

Hunter said, "When you get hit, you just run down to first base. Sometimes, if you are hit in the back, you are gasping for air the whole way, but if you stop, you are a wuss. You can't do that. So you just take it like a man. After you get hit by a pitch in the back, you go in the family room after the game, and all your little cousins are in there, and they run up to you and slap you on the back and you think, 'Oh, God, please don't do that.' But you can't yell at them because they are kids. You can't let little kids think you are in pain."

Baker said, "We hit Prince Fielder on purpose in the minor leagues, in Beloit. He hit a ball that went so far, he hit it ten years ago, and it just landed the other day. He wouldn't run until it landed, so we were waiting and waiting and waiting for him to run. So next time up, we hit him in the shin. He reached down and pretended to brush off his shin, like a fly had landed on it. Then he gave our pitcher the death stare. Our pitcher was scared."

The pain is excruciating. "Anyone who says it doesn't hurt is insane," Boesch said. "It hurts, but adrenaline helps. The game is on national TV. Everyone sees you. Don't show it."

By showing pain, you are showing respect to the pitcher.

"You don't want to give that satisfaction to the pitcher," Diaz said. "He might think his stuff is good that day. But if he hits you with 96 [mph], and you just walk to first, he might have a doubt in his mind. He might say, 'Maybe my stuff isn't that good.'" Santangelo said, "I've seen pitchers get rattled when you don't show it hurt. You get them off their game."

No matter how hard you get hit, no matter where, says Jones, "You can't rub it, don't rub it, don't rub it. You are a major leaguer. You can't rub it. Go somewhere where the cameras can't see you or else the fans will be all over you."

And so will your teammates.

"[Padres first baseman] Yonder [Alonso] got hit in the back;

he walked through the clubhouse and everyone would slap him on the back where it really hurt, that's what five-year-olds we really are," said Baker. "If you limp through the clubhouse after getting hit, three or four teammates will be limping right behind you, mocking you. Spring training 2009, my last at bat, I got hit right in the ass with a sinker. I had two half moons on each butt cheek, half of a baseball on each butt cheek. It was like I had stood in front of a pitching machine, and let it hit me right up in there. I looked so funny. My teammates railed on me for about three days, but you have to take it. That was a very comedic bruise."

But it's not funny. In some cases, the pain is greater than the machismo.

"I got hit in April by [Neftali] Feliz in 30-degree weather at 100 mph," Boesch said. "I had to take a moment at the plate. There was no way I was sprinting to first base after that . . . I'm sure once Will Rhymes came to, his teammates had a lot of fun with him after that."

LaRoche smiled and said, "After I got hit in the knee by Josh Johnson, I had to take a knee. I didn't care what my teammates said. Let 'em laugh all they want. I need a second here."

> *Fear of the ball is the deep dark secret in baseball that players don't talk about. It is a crossroads for players. You can't have courage unless you're afraid. If you don't have fear, there's nothing to be brave about. Everyone fears that little white sports car.*
>
> —Joe Torre

To acknowledge fear of the ball is to acknowledge weakness, which is not in a player's constitution. Only on occasion, and usually with humor, does anyone acknowledge fear publicly.

"The most scared I've ever been was facing Erick Threets of the White Sox in the minor leagues," said Baker. "He was a big left-hander throwing from three-quarters, and he was all over the place. I got way in the back of the box, like Henry Rowen-gartner from *Rookie of the Year*. I was not up there to get hit in the face. I had some fear."

Almost every player does, to some degree. But they can deal with it.

"Cody Ross got hit in the face against us when he squared to bunt," Diaz said. "The next day, he led off the game with a home run. Incredible. It is in our DNA to get back in the box."

Outfielder Carlos Quentin seemingly has no fear. He has been hit more than 100 times in less than 800 games, more times than Mantle, Willie Mays, and Hank Aaron were hit in 8,691 games combined.

"Quentin is not going to move," said Baker. "He's not afraid of anything. He is the epitome of the alpha male in baseball. He is not going to show weakness. He gets hit, and he doesn't care. In the minor leagues, we used to hit him on purpose. It's just his style of hitting. He defends home plate, and he does so in an offensive way. He comes from the Stanford way of doing things; team overrides everything, anything to win, any way to get on."

Hinske shook his head and said, "Reed Johnson and Chase Utley are that way—they do not budge up there. That doesn't make me any less of a man or any less of a player than them, but they don't have a flinch mechanism at the plate. I do. I will jump out of the way."

Kendall will not.

"I just got used to it," he said. "I got hit. I went down to first base. If you have fear, you will never have success in this game. It's a part of the game. But the game has changed. If you get a bruise now, you come out of the game. That's not the way I played.

My old man [Fred Kendall] played in the big leagues. They played their asses off back then [in the late '60s and '70s]. You play with bumps and bruises. I've had concussions. For six to eight months a year, you get the [expletive] beat out of your body. It's hot, it's cold, and you get hit by pitches. I was the guy that snapped his ankle, started a lot of fights, and got hit a lot."

The Pirates' Sean Rodriguez gets hit a lot, too.

"He's never afraid," said veteran infielder Elliot Johnson. "He gets hit all the time. And we never have to wonder who that is yelling from our bench to take one for the team. It's Sean."

"For me, it goes back to Little League: my dad taught me, you will do whatever it takes to get on base, and win a game. Anything," Rodriguez said. "There are times when you're going to have to wear it, so wear it. There is a fear factor, but you can't have any fear. You have to get back in there. So you get back in there. I want to get back in there and get that pitcher's ass for what he did to me. I scream out "*el equipo*," which means 'team' in Spanish. I don't always yell it. I don't yell it when Evan [Longoria] is at the plate. I don't yell it when the count is 2-0 or 2-1. But if the count is 0-1 or 0-2, I will scream it, even at Evan."

Diaz said, "If I get hit on an 0-2 or 1-2 pitch, it's like, *Yes!* Or if you are struggling, and you're facing a guy you can't hit, and you get hit, it doesn't hurt and you're not scared."

It really does hurt, and they really are scared, but major leaguers are able to deal with it because that is their job, and it is what they have been conditioned to do. When the rest of us would be running for our lives, they move closer to the plate, dig in, and get hit again.

"With baseball players, you take one of two options, fight or flight," Baker said. "Most players choose the fight response." Diaz said, "I would say that of all the players, major leaguers are the most insane. Back in Little League, when the smart kids got hit by a pitch, and it really hurt, they went on to do something else with their lives. We got back in the box. There's a fine line between being brave and being stupid, but this is who we are."

Shelley Duncan's father, Dave, played in the major leagues, and so did his brother, Chris. They grew up in the game, which is why Shelley can say, "Pain threshold is different for everyone. I always say, 'It's just a baseball. How can it hurt you? It's just a baseball. What does it weigh, 6 ounces? How can anything that weighs 6 ounces hurt you?' For what I get to do for a living, I think I can put up with getting hit with a ball once a month."

Baker, a catcher, gets hit nightly by foul tips, balls in the dirt, and pitches.

"I have just come to the understanding with myself that I'm going to get hit," he said. "But I weigh 210 pounds and the ball weighs 6 ounces. So, in that matchup, I like my chances."

4. SOUNDS OF THE GAME

When You Hear "You Suck" for the 30,000th Time, You Tune It Out

When I stopped playing, what I missed most was the sounds of the ballpark. For years after I retired, I heard those sounds in my head before I went to sleep.

—Stan Musial

IF SOMEONE apprehended and blindfolded and transported to you a secret location that could not be traced, as did the Albanians when they kidnapped Liam Neeson's daughter in the movie *Taken,* the last place your abductor would choose is a major league stadium. The sounds of the game are unmistakably present every night, in every ballpark. They are unique to baseball. Some are loud, some subtle. After sight, hearing is the most acute of the senses; it helps create a fan experience unlike in any other sport. Close your eyes and listen, and you'll know what park you're in, which team is winning, and which pitcher is dealing.

Roger Clemens said he loved going to the Astrodome to "listen" to Nolan Ryan warm up in the bullpen before a game, the gunshot sound that Ryan's 100-mph fastball would make when it collided with the catcher's mitt. Chipper Jones said he loved the clatter sound made by Bobby Cox's metal spikes on concrete in the runway to the dugout, a sure sign that another major league game was about to start.

"My favorite sound is that little *click* you hear when the hitter knocks the batting donut off his bat in the on-deck circle," said veteran outfielder Lance Berkman. "When I hear that, I know it's time for me to hit."

There are three places from which the most distinct sounds come—the plate, the mound, and the stands—but the sounds come from everywhere. "I've always liked the sound around second base when there's a steal," said outfielder Sam Fuld. "The runner is sliding, the ball hits the glove, the runner hits the bag. [It's not the same violent sound], but all that commotion must be similar to what goes on at the line of scrimmage in an NFL game."

Former outfielder Matt Diaz said, "I love the sound of footsteps. With the big guys, you hear that *thump, thump, thump*—the louder the footsteps, the slower the guy. Andrew McCutchen, you never hear his feet, it's like he's floating. When he's going after a ball, it's like *ah, ah, ah*. When that sound gets really loud, you move aside and let him catch it."

Outfielder Reed Johnson said it's hard to hear another outfielder running at you in the heat of a game in a loud ballpark. "You learn to glance over and look off the guy next to you," he said. "I played next to Vernon Wells for five years [in Toronto], and we never said a word to each other because we always knew where we were, and who could make the play."

Astros outfielder Carlos Gomez yells all the time on the bases. "He is always making noise," said Angels pitcher C. J. Wilson. "As soon as he hits the ball, he's running to first and he's making these motorboat noises as he runs. And he's yelling. I think at himself, but I'm not sure."

Catcher John Baker said, "Some guys were just born in the wrong country. Carlos Gomez should be in the NFL. He is so big and so fast, and he makes so much noise as soon as he starts running. He's like a train chugging down the track."

Gomez explained himself, saying, "I am still a kid out there, I still do things like I did when I was 12. I used to watch track-and-field guys when they ran, what their faces looked like, the sounds they made. When I run, I'm counting every step. Not like one, two, three, four . . . I'm telling myself, 'One more step, one more step' until I reach the next base."

And when runners reach base, the conversations begin. "Dunner [former first baseman Adam Dunn] is the best talker in the world," said outfielder Jeff Francoeur. "When I'm on first, he'll say to me, 'You don't have a big enough lead.' Or, 'You have too big a lead.' He gets pissed when you make him jump off the bag and get in fielding position. It really pisses him off when you hit a double, and he has to trail you to second. He's yelling at you the whole way for making him run to second."

White Sox first baseman Adam LaRoche laughed and said, "Adam will not shut up. He is always funny. He rarely talks about baseball. He will talk to whoever is around him. All the umpires know not to get within 50 yards of him. If there's no one around, I'm convinced Adam will talk to himself."

Dunn smiled and said, "I'm not going to be bored out there. When I'm bored, I'm out of here."

There are conversations going on everywhere. "Miguel Tejada talked to himself, or his imaginary friend, the whole game," Baker said. "I think what comes out of his mouth shuts out the voice inside of his head."

And there are conversations that take place in the dugout

every night. "I draw a line in our dugout," said A's manager Bob
Melvin with a smile. "Some players who are not playing that day
know that they are not allowed to cross that line and come over
and talk to me during the game because they are going to drive
me crazy about not being in the lineup that day. Josh Reddick is
one of those guys."

The Tigers' Miguel Cabrera always plays, and always talks.
"He is a lovable, funny guy," Wilson said. "Guys rub people the
wrong way with what they say in the field. Not Miggy. He's always messing with the Latin guys on the other team. [The Rangers'] Elvis Andrus was always making fun of him. He would call
him fat, and Miggy would fire back."

There are constant conversations between teammates, but not
always in words; it can be in sounds. "It's very hard to hear your
fellow infielders during the course of a game. When you see a
shortstop and second baseman move closer to each other before a
play, it's so they can talk to each other when you can't communi-
cate with your hands," said second baseman Dan Uggla. "That's
why there's a lot of whistling going on to get someone's attention.
Our outfielders whistle to our infielders all the time. Rossie [catcher
David Ross, an ex-teammate] is the best whistler ever. You can
hear his whistle from miles away."

Veteran manager Davey Johnson, who played second base on
pennant-winning teams in Baltimore in the 1960s and '70s, said,
"A lot of the communication out there is very subtle. I called the
coverage with visual signs, but sometimes [shortstop] Luis [Apari-
cio] would want a verbal command, and I'd know what he wanted
just by his facial expression. When I went behind first base to
catch a pop-up, Boog [Powell, the Orioles first baseman] always
knew my voice. There can be 50,000 people screaming bloody
murder out there, but the only thing you hear is the guy's voice
that you need to hear on that play."

The worst sound on a baseball field, Baker said, "is the sound when someone gets hit by a pitch. That dull thud sound, you're going to have a bruise tomorrow. That slap sound, you probably broke your wrist. That slapping sound, the skin-on-skin sound, you know it's really bad. The worst sound of all is when a guy gets hit in the head."

J. T. Snow was once hit in the head by the scariest pitcher maybe ever, Randy Johnson. "I was lying in the dirt, blood gushing from my eye," Snow said. "It felt like I'd been coldcocked, like in a fight. All I could hear was my wife screaming in the stands."

Rays third baseman Evan Longoria smiled and said, "The worst sound is the sound of the ball hitting a guy's cup. It happened to me the other day. If you can hear it, that very loud tap, you know it's bad. Only the men can hear it. When you hear it, everyone just ducks their heads and hopes that the guy is okay. We all know what it feels like to take one in the cup."

The Sounds at the Plate

When it's my turn to hit, the quietest place on earth is home plate.

—Ted Williams

Hitting a baseball is the hardest skill in sports. Remarkable concentration is required to hit a ball traveling 95 mph. Tiger Woods is incensed when a single camera clicks during his backswing. When a tennis player is getting ready to serve the ball, fans are asked to cease conversation. But when a hitter is trying to make contact with Aroldis Chapman's 100-mph heater, the crowd is urged to go wild. Yet inner silence is imperative for the hitter.

"When you are locked in at the plate, you can't hear a thing," said Francoeur. "But when you are struggling, you hear *every-thing* . . . especially when you're in Philly."

Infielder Mark Reynolds said, "I try to block everything out when I'm up there, like Kevin Costner in *For Love of the Game.* The less you hear, the better. If you hear people, you can't hit."

Diaz said, "I hear everything until the pitcher goes in his motion, then my senses shut down, and all I hear is a buzz." Baker said, "Players misidentify the sound. They hear it, but it's ambient noise. The sound that is more intimidating is with the smaller crowd. In Miami, you could hear everything that was said. Something that is very private becomes very public when there are only fifty people there. With 50,000 fans, when you walk to the plate, you can't *not* hear that, but it is white noise, like the noise that makes a baby sleep. You hear it, but you don't notice it."

Uggla said, "When I go to the plate, there is just a whole lot of nothing going on. My mind just kind of goes silent. A few times, you will hear that one fan that everyone can hear from home plate to center field. And you'll ask yourself, 'Why am I hearing that guy?'"

Dunn said, "You don't hear anything. If you do, they've won. That's the home field advantage."

Though as the hitter tries to keep his concentration, tries to stay focused, sounds still interrupt it. Reynolds said, "I hate it when the catcher and umpire get in a conversation during an AB. I step out of the box and want to tell them, 'Hey, shut the fuck up, I'm trying to concentrate here.'"

Infielder Elliot Johnson agreed, saying, "When they are both talking back there, I just look back at them with a look that says, 'Hey, are you done yet? I'm trying to hit here.'"

And then there are the ball and strike calls by umpires. Some are loud, others soft.

"There's so much sensory focus," Wilson said. "When Tim

McClelland is umpiring, your ears are turned up because he takes so long to make a call. I love Tom Hallion's strike call: *byyyyy-aaaaa*. And it's not even strike three. Then he throws a punch. I got T-shirts made that say, 'Go for the Punch.' He has the best call. I look forward to hearing that call even when it's against our hitters. I love Jim Joyce's call: the *eeeeeee* scream. When we go up and say hello to him, we say, 'How is it going, Jim-eeeeeee?'" Baker said, "When Joyce or Hallion call you out, and do a dance behind you, that's one thing. It's worse when Mc-Clelland calls you out and you can barely hear him."

And then there are the catchers that like to talk to the hitter. Francoeur said, "[A. J.] Pierzynski talks the most. We talk Florida football. Clemson football. The nicest is Joe Mauer."

Dunn said with a smile, "Chad Moeller is the worst. He won't shut up behind the plate. He's talking while the pitch is coming. I have to look at him and say, 'Will you please shut up? Don't talk to me.' It really bugs me. With him, I'm praying for a play at the plate."

Baker said, "I talk a lot to the hitters. I have nine-inning conversations with Brian McCann. But Lance Berkman is the best. He will talk to you the entire at bat, even when the pitch is coming to the plate. He once stepped in the box and told me that he got a new dog, a Lab. He said, 'He's eating my socks, my sheets.' And then he'll say, after the first pitch, 'That pitch was down, wasn't it?' Then he will continue to tell me about his dog during a major league at bat. That's how relaxed Lance is. That's why he's such a great hitter."

With great hitters, the sound of the ball coming off their bat makes, some say, a different sound.

"That's my favorite sound on the baseball field, when a big hitter hits the ball really hard, it makes a *pluck* sound," said former manager Dusty Baker. "Henry Aaron's bat made that sound. So did Barry Bonds's. But the guy that all my guys would come back to the dugout and say the ball exploded off his bat was Fred Mc-Griff. There's no sound like that. That *pluck* sound is when a guy scalds that ball. You can hear that sound all over the park."

Pierzynski said, "Miguel Cabrera's bat makes the loudest sound. That's easy. He hit a ball last year that went so far—about 520 feet to dead center field—my ears are still ringing from that. After the inning, I had to go get my ears checked to see if they were bleeding."

Former pitcher Curt Schilling said, "Delmon Young, when he was 20, made the loudest sound I've ever heard. We had our backs to the cage, four or five guys went through, then we heard this sound. I turned around and it was Delmon Young. I'd never heard a sound that loud. I thought he'd win a batting title."

Elliot Johnson said, "I played with Delmon, and I played with Elijah Dukes, and the sound off of Dukes's bat was louder. But the loudest I've ever heard is Jose Bautista. I could turn my head to the side and tell you when he was taking batting practice. He uses an ash bat. Ash bats are louder than maple bats."

Dunn said, "[Dayan] Viciedo [of the White Sox] makes the loudest sound. I can tell you if he's hitting in our group, or way over on Field 4. It sounds like a cannon when he hits the ball. He swings so hard. I'd blow out every muscle in my back if I swung the bat that hard."

But according to most players, the loudest sound comes off the bat of Josh Hamilton.

"When you're walking to the tunnel, and you hear the sound off Josh Hamilton's bat, you say, 'What the hell is that?' It sounds like a gunshot," Baker said. "And he was hitting with Nelson Cruz and Mike Napoli, guys with a lot of power. Mike Trout makes a lot of noise, also. He doesn't start his swing until it's so late, later than anyone, that quickness creates serious noise."

C. J. Wilson said, "It depends what type of bat you use. An

ash bat has more of a whip sound to it; a maple bat has more of a crack. There is no sound coming off the bat like the one off Josh's bat. That's partly because he uses a really heavy bat, 33 ounces. It's sort of a smashing sound. Most guys have a little click. It's like his sound lasts much longer than other guys'. It reverberates more than other guys'. It echoes. When he squares it up, you can hear it from 100 feet away. And when you're in an enclosed place, like the batting cage in Detroit, it is crazy loud when he's hitting." Diaz said, "There's nothing like the sound off Josh Hamilton's bat. He uses such a heavy bat. It's much more dense. It resonates."

Francoeur said, "I played with Chipper [Jones]. I played with Billy [Butler]. I played with Josh. There is nothing like the sound that's made when Josh crushes a baseball."

LaRoche said, "I could swing Josh's bat and make a similar noise even though he swings the bat 100 mph faster than I do. But I wouldn't make that sound nearly as often as he does."

Berkman shook his head in disbelief.

"I think it's psychosomatic," he said. "I can't tell the difference. Josh Hamilton's sound is no different from the sound of Miguel Cabrera, Albert Pujols, Matt Holliday, and Prince Fielder. It's been that way forever in baseball. Old-timers said, 'Oh, you should have heard the sound made by the bat of' . . . then fill in the blank. If you took the ten best hitters in baseball, put a blindfold on me, I couldn't tell the difference between the sound of any of them."

The Sounds on the Mound

I knew I was in trouble on the mound tonight. I could hear the crowd.

—Roger Clemens

Remarkable concentration is a requirement to be a major league pitcher. The night in the 2000 World Series when Clemens picked up the barrel of Mike Piazza's broken bat and threw it at Piazza is the perfect example of that focus: Clemens mouthed the words, "I thought it was the ball," meaning he thought the bat was the ball, and that's why he picked it up and threw it at Piazza. A convenient excuse? Maybe. But when pitchers get in a zone when they are on the mound, they have no idea what's going on. They need that silence.

"I don't want to hear a sound out there, I don't hear a sound," said Rangers pitcher Derek Holland. "Have you ever seen the movie *For Love of the Game*? I try to watch it the night before every start. I don't stand on the mound and whisper, 'Hear the Mechanism' to myself like Costner did. But I get so locked, I can't hear anything. The only sound I hear is when I turn to say something to an infielder, which really annoys them."

Wilson said, "I don't hear a thing, I hear nothing out there. But when a dude really squares one against you, then you can hear it, you know and you drop your head and say, 'Please, go foul, or hit a bird.' When a player hits a home run on the road, and the place is really loud, and then the place just goes silent, that's the big noise: the absence of noise. It's like when a record skips, or some guy walks into a party who's not supposed to be there."

Nationals pitcher Drew Storen said, "I don't hear anything from the stands; it's like from *For Love of the Game*. But I can hear my infielders. I can hear what's being said in the dugout. It's fascinating. As players, we have a sense of whose voices are what. We hear what we need to hear, and we don't pay attention to what we don't need. It's very difficult to get our outfielders' attention from the bullpen, but they can hear things from the dugout because that's where they need to be listening. As players, we know the sounds of the game. You know when there's a fly ball and the fans yell, 'Oh,' like it's gone? As players, we aren't fooled by that sound. We know that's a routine fly ball to center."

And yet, the mound can be a very noisy place.

"Pitchers are out there grunting and snorting. Jake Peavy is the best, he's hilarious," Wilson said. "He's always yelling at himself on the mound. He's yelling, 'Dang it, Jake, that's terrible.' [Reliever] Grant Balfour is always yelling at himself, also. He grunts all the time. I will yell a loud obscenity once in a while. I'll drop an f-bomb. At that point, there is no volume control out there. It's like, 'Whoops, sorry to the kids in the front row.'"

Peavy smiled and said, "I try not to yell, I try not to swear, but at seven o'clock every night, I turn into someone different. I'm out there trying to focus. I'm competing. I can't control myself, but I have three little boys. I want them to be able to watch their daddy pitch without hearing all the yelling. Greg Maddux made me feel good. He would say one bad word all the time when he pitched. I just try to say, "God bless it.' But I wear my emotions on a sleeve. I'm conscious of it. I love to compete. I am not a crazy animal. But it's been eleven to twelve years of this. I don't think I'm going to change. And I'm not going to apologize."

Dunn smiled and said, "I make fun of Jake, I mock him. I can't even make the sound he makes when he's out there—it will hurt my throat. We do an over/under on when he's going to first yell at himself. I usually set it at about five and a half pitches. He's a clown."

Diaz said, "In the minor leagues, Peavy broke my bat. I singled up the middle and he yelled at me, 'Are you going to take that?' I said, 'Yes. I need all the help I can get off Jake Peavy.'"

Baker said, "[Chris] Carpenter and [Roy] Halladay are always yelling at themselves. I saw Carpenter give up a hit to a guy—a guy who was just called up—in a simulated game, and Carpenter was screaming into his glove as the guy was running to first. It wasn't very nice language. Halladay is the same way. I hit a grounder up the middle off him a couple of years ago, and he bore a hole in my face with his eyes, then he screamed at me. That was a good feeling: make a guy that good that mad." Baker added, "Kip Wells yells on the mound all the time. Or he'd really grunt, that Serena Williams grunt. We'd mess with him and tell him that he only screamed when he threw his breaking ball, so he started screaming on his fastball. Jason Marquis told me last year that he was going to start screaming when he let the ball go, just yell 'strike three,' just to mess up the hitter."

Pitchers make sounds with their pitches. Ex-Dodgers catcher Paul Lo Duca once said that Eric Gagne's changeup spun so quickly and tightly, "It would rip your shirt." And it made noise.

"Some pitchers, you can hear the ball coming, it's spinning so fast," Wilson said. "It makes a sizzling sound, it comes in so hot. [Alexi] Ogando's ball makes that sound. His stuff is so filthy. It has backspin on it. [The Angels'] Garrett Richards is the same way. The ball is halfway to you, and you think, 'Oh, shit, here it comes,' it's making so much noise. Rick Ankiel was like no one else. When he threw that curveball, you could hear it spinning from the dugout. It was disgusting. His curveball is the loudest I've ever heard."

Reynolds said, "You can hear a really tight slider. It sounds like a big insect flying by your ear. Back in the day, you could hear Peavy's slider. And [John] Smoltz's slider. They were loud."

Dunn said, "It happened to me this spring with [the White Sox's] Nate Jones. I was facing him on the back field. I couldn't see the ball, but I could hear it coming. I thought, 'That one *sounded* really hard.' It makes a sound, a buzz, like a pissed-off bumble-bee."

Baker said, "With [veteran right-hander] Josh Johnson, it sounds like a missile is coming at you."

LaRoche said, "When [Adam] Wainwright throws his curveball, I hear the pop when he lets it go."

Fuld said, "When [Justin] Verlander throws that curveball, it is spinning so fast, you can hear it. He just has more revolutions on it that anyone else. But the sound you hear after he throws that curveball is even louder: the *whoosh* of the bat when you swing and miss."

The Sounds of the Crowd

I listen to the fans, But when you hear "You suck" for the 30,000th time, you tune it out.

—Adam Dunn

Baseball fans are different from those in any other sport. There are so many of them, they are so close to the field, there is a game every night, the game moves so slowly, there is so much dead time, so much time to rag on the players. And even though the players are able to block out the sounds of the fans when on the mound or at the plate, an outfielder can stand in one place for thirty minutes at a time, with the fans right behind him, screaming at him. That's why there is more heckling going on in baseball than in the other sports.

"A couple of places there is great animosity for you: Wrigley Field and San Francisco," Berkman said. "You get the feeling there that they genuinely hate you. They are very uncreative there, you know, they usually just say, 'You suck.' Or, they call me fat."

Fuld, who is 5'8", said, "You can hear the fans in Oakland and

Toronto. I get yelled at, especially about my height. You know, the usual, 'Hey, Fuld, stand up, we can't see you.'"

Baker said, "You can hear people yelling at you, especially when you're going poorly. You can hear the three people screaming at you, 'Baker, you suck.' At Dodger Stadium, 50,000 are screaming at you. Barry Bonds said you have to be pretty good to have 50,000 yelling at you. I think it's worse when three guys are, and you can hear every word they say."

But every ballpark is different.

"Your ears play tricks on you," Wilson said. "The acoustics are so loud in some parks. Like Tampa, it's so loud in there even when there are only 10,000 in the stands. There's a fan in the stands with the cowbell, you can hear him. There's an old Rays fan in an old Rays jersey, you can listen to the game on the radio, and hear his voice. You know why players wear warm-up jackets in the bullpen? It's so the uneducated fans don't know them, and can't yell their name. It is like, 'Hey, you,' or 'Hey, brown-haired pitcher,' instead of, 'Hey, Wilson.' But in Detroit, they are very clever. When the Rangers had Eric Gagne, they'd yell, 'Hey, French Tickler, how are you?' It was hilarious. One city, which I won't mention, they are not inventive. They have the worst heckler there. He yells at the right fielder the whole game, he just yells his name. Really? Is that it? Is that all you have?"

A lot depends on where you are playing.

"In spring training, you can hear the left fielder cough from the pitcher's mound," Wilson said. "But in the regular season, when you are in a packed ballpark in a stressful situation, you can only hear the roar of the crowd. In quieter places, you can hear a fan in the upper deck. It's funny, but my brother comes to all the games I start. His voice cuts like a knife. When he yells, 'Yes, C. J.,' I can hear him from wherever he is sitting. I laugh my ass off. He weighs 140 pounds, and I can hear him in a crowd of 40,000. It's a genetic thing."

Some visiting players have become favorites of the home crowd. Several years ago, the fans in the right-field stands in Oakland became favorites of Francoeur because they were so passionate, and so funny. So, during one game in Oakland, he wrapped a baseball in bacon, threw it to the Bleacher Creatures in right field. "I call them the Bacon Crew," Francoeur said. "Last year, I bought them all a bunch of hot dogs during the game, and they started cheering me. Then I bought them pizza. At the end of spring training [2013], they came to an exhibition game in Camelback just to cheer for me. I got together with those guys for an hour in the parking lot after a game this spring. We just cooked some bacon."

Francoeur said he hears no sounds when at the plate, but he hears everything in the outfield because "it takes a lot more focus to hit than it does to play the outfield. I am so confident in my ability out there. I hear everything, but I can still focus completely on the game."

Diaz agreed. He hears the fans when he plays the outfield. In Philadelphia, he used to get razzed, as do all outfielders, until a few years ago, he said, "when I leg-whipped the Red Man. This guy came running out in the field dressed in a red spandex outfit. I was considering giving him a full-steam spear, but he was slightly built, and for a second, I thought it might be a woman. So I leg-whipped him to the ground, then the security guys clobbered him. The security guys gave me a security T-shirt and an ID badge. The next Halloween, I went dressed as a security man. It was a nice night at the park. The next time I went there, I got a standing ovation from the fans. Then they heckled me. They'd scream, 'You don't hit the ball as hard as you hit our fans.' The fans in Philadelphia are very creative."

That's what Dunn is looking for.

"I listen to the fans," he said. "I don't want to miss anything. I am listening when I'm at first base. I am listening for something funny. I am willing to laugh if they say something funny."

Elliot Johnson laughed and said, "I heard a guy yell this: 'Elliot Johnson, Elliot Johnson, I Googled you, and the reply I got was, "Why?"' I turned and gave him the thumbs-up. That was pretty funny. He made me laugh. There's no telling what you might hear at the ballpark."

5. SUPERSTITIONS

There Are a Lot of Hits in That Shower

ELLIOT JOHNSON, THE journeyman infielder, always places a piece of Super Bubble grape-flavored bubble gum in his mouth when he runs on the field to play defense. When his team is batting, he discards the grape, and replaces it with Super Bubble watermelon-flavored bubble gum because, he says, with certainty, "The hits are in the watermelon gum."

The hits are in the watermelon gum. It is preposterous, of course, but Johnson actually believes it, which, in the crazy world of baseball, is all that matters. He got a couple of hits in a minor league game a few years ago while chewing watermelon gum, so now it is his best chance to get two hits tonight. Johnson acknowledges that it is also "an oral fixation, to some degree," but after this many years, he is superstitious about it. And superstitions remain as alive today as they did twenty years ago when Turk Wendell would pitch without wearing socks, chewed black licorice every inning he pitched, then brushed his teeth after every inning, and would not step on the mound until his catcher was in a crouch.

"When I got to Atlanta [in 2013]," said Johnson, who began

that season with the Royals, "they didn't have the flavored gum that I *need*. I was pretty upset. But one of the clubhouse kids found some for me at a store, and I was as happy as could be." He laughed, but he wasn't kidding, when he said, "And that first night, of course, I got a hit."

And he got the hit because of the gum. Baseball is the hardest game in the world to play, so excruciatingly difficult, in fact, that players will do *anything* to make them *feel* like they have a better chance to get a hit off Clayton Kerhsaw, or get Miguel Cabrera out in a key situation. It's all about feeling comfortable, prepared, and confident, and if having the right gum or the right pair of socks or freshly brushed teeth are going to give a player a better chance to succeed, then that's what he's going to have. It's the ultimate game of skill, and its players always are searching for good luck.

"Baseball is a very funny game," said veteran outfielder Luke Scott. "If one little thing doesn't go right, it can throw you off. If you don't complete all your superstitions, it can really throw you off, and make you look like you have never played the game before."

"It is taboo to talk about it: players are superstitious about being superstitious," said catcher John Baker. "It is like, 'If I let you in on my little secret, I might not get a couple of hits.'"

So now instead of calling it a superstition, players will call what they do "a routine," but it's semantics: the fact remains that they do weird things every day because they feel they *have to* or else it will bring them bad luck. Former pitcher Scott Erickson used to wear all black on the days he pitched, and spoke to no one those days—"We called it the 'Day of Death,'" teammate Kevin Tapani once said—but now players aren't as obvious about their superstitions or routines, and don't publicize them—they even disguise them. But I have found a few, and I have determined that these superstitions or routines can be classified in five distinct categories: Random Acts of Strangeness, Clothing and Uniforms, Food and Drink, Hygiene, and, all by himself, reliever Randy Choate.

"You can spend a lifetime talking about players' superstitions," said veteran first baseman Adam LaRoche. "My only superstition is to have no superstition. I don't wear the same thing, or eat the same thing, if I get three hits. I can wear any of the eight pairs of cleats that I have in my locker. I borrow people's bats all the time, different models than the ones I use, it doesn't matter. I am jealous, to some degree, of the guys that get in the same routine every day. I have never been able to do that. I tried, then I finally quit trying. But I don't want anything holding me back. I don't want anything weighing on me. What if I wanted to go to my son's game, but I missed it because I have to go to the same sub shop for lunch every day at the same time? How am I going to explain that to my wife?"

Random Acts of Strangeness

"Have you seen what [pitcher] Edward Mujica does?" pitcher Jason Motte said of his former Cardinals teammate.

"He says he's not superstitious, he says this is all part of his routine . . . yeah, right," said Choate, then-teammate reliever, with a laugh. "He always has to be in the same spot in the bullpen with two outs in the fourth inning of every game. Then, in the fifth inning, he always digs a hole at the front end of the bullpen mound, then he spits a half cup of red Gatorade into the hole. It has to be red. He also likes to put his sleeve in my coat jacket every night in the bullpen. I'm not sure why . . . and they say that I'm all screwed up?"

Maybe it's a reliever thing.

"[Left-hander] Sean Burnett always carries a poker chip in his back pocket when he pitches," said Nationals reliever Drew Storen, a former teammate. "But it works for him."

"[Veteran reliever] Kyle Farnsworth hated it when anyone flipped him the ball," LaRoche said. "So, every chance I would get, I'd flip him the ball. He would let it hit off his glove, fall to the ground, then he would throw it to the umpire, and ask for a new ball."

And then there's former Tigers reliever Jose Valverde.

"Papa Grande would always come out of the bullpen with a mouthful of water," said ex-Tigers reliever Phil Coke. "He would spit it out, an equal amount to each side, then slap his thigh with his glove. With his hat in one hand and his glove in the other, he would run to the mound. On the way, he would never step on any line on the field. I mean, not just the foul line, any line. When the grass is cut diagonally, he'd never step on a line in the grass."

Maybe it's a pitcher thing.

"Every night before I pitch, I *have* to play Nintendo hockey," said Rangers left-hander Derek Holland. "Every night before I pitch, I *have* to watch the movie *For Love of The Game*, the Kevin Costner movie. I watch the same part every time, but never the whole movie. I've never seen the whole movie, and I never will until I retire. People tell me how it ends, but I don't care, I won't watch it until I retire. But I have to watch it every night before I pitch. It's what helps get me ready to pitch."

If it's not a movie, it's a song.

"I know with Andy Pettitte, guaranteed, on the days he pitched, he would listen to the entire *Rocky* soundtrack," said Scott, who was a teammate of Pettitte's with the Astros. "That's like clockwork. It pumps him up. There's no one around, just him and *Rocky*."

Veteran outfielder Torii Hunter said of a former teammate, Bobby Abreu, "At 6:30 every night for a 7:05 game, Bobby would put his headphones on and play that 'September' song, you know, 'Do you remember/the twenty-first night of September.' Same song every night, but only when he was starting. He had to listen to it before every game. After he listened to that song, he'd be smiling, he would be all happy, he would be slapping everyone's hand around him. It's what he needed to get ready to play that night."

Journeyman utility guy Greg Dobbs, a veteran of eleven major league seasons, shook his head and said, "What I don't understand are these guys, right before the game, that have their headphones on. And they listen to the same song over and over again. The same song! It's like they are in a trance. The same song for 162 consecutive games! I don't know how they do it without going crazy. It's nuts! [Closer Steve] Cishek does that. [Reliever] Mike Dunn does the same thing. I feel like going to them and saying, "Dude, listen to something else, please. It's not going to hurt you. You will be fine.' But it's what they need, it's what they do. They think I'm strange with what I do. And I think they are strange."

Reds third baseman Todd Frazier doesn't listen to music; he sings and chants before every game he starts.

"Part of my routine every day is to go into the trainers' room and do the roll call," Frazier said. "So, if [pitcher] Alfredo Simon is in there, I'll walk in and sing and clap, 'Alfred-o, Si-mon.' Then he has to raise his hand. When he raises his hand, I stop. Then our trainer, Paul Lassard, will yell, 'What's wrong with Frazier?' and whoever is in the trainers' room will yell together, 'He's a bum!' [Reds coach] Billy Hatcher taught us the song they used to sing about the Big Red Machine, they called it 'Red Hot.' So every day, I put this red-hot cream on my arm, and I sing a rap song that goes something like, 'Because we're the Reds, we're red hot.' I do that three times, and we're ready to go play. But the last thing I do before I go out on the field every night is go to our masseuse, Mickey. And I sing to her, 'Hey, Mickey, you're so fine.' And she says, 'Thank you, let's go.' And we're off to play."

The last thing Chipper Jones did before every game "was to play computer solitaire until 6:55 every night, then he went straight to the dugout," LaRoche said. "It's what got him ready."

"[Padres outfielder] Carlos Quentin does all sorts of things," said former White Sox first baseman Paul Konerko. "He has this spray, he calls it an 'aura spray.' It helps him feel better about himself. It gives him some kind of an aura for the game. He doesn't spray it on himself like cologne, he sprays it up in the air, then walks under it, so it just kind of falls on him, like an aura. He brings his own sheets when he goes on the road to a hotel. He has special sheets—like wearing a bracelet—only the sheets cover his whole body for good luck."

When Adam Dunn was the DH for the White Sox, the last thing he said he did minutes before every game was "take four pieces of sugarless gum as I stand on the top step of the dugout. Everyone on our team knows I do this. I chew them into a nice ball, then I spit it out. Then—using my hand as a bat—I swat the wad of gum out toward the field. Everyone on our team gets out of the way because they know I'm swatting my gum wad out onto the field. Tonight, [Orioles third baseman] Manny Machado will have to start the game by walking down the third-base line and tossing a big wad of gum off the field. I don't know why I do that. I have forever."

What Dunn has never done, he said, is stand in the on-deck circle.

"I don't like the feeling of having the warning track under me," he said. "It's not the same consistency of dirt that there is in the batter's box, so I don't want to feel that before I go to the plate. I stand on the grass where it's soft. I have never been in the on-deck circle."

Neither has the Royals' Alex Gordon.

"He will not, he always stands on the grass next to the circle," said Elliot Johnson, a former teammate. "You can see his footprints. He wears down the grass, and they had to re-sod it because he won't stand in the on-deck circle dirt. The groundskeeper has to hate him."

The batter's box always has been a place for rituals, from Mike Hargrove (the Human Rain Delay) to Nomar Garciaparra (he adjusted his batting gloves, tapped his toe, etc., after every pitch) to the Red Sox's Pablo Sandoval, whose pre–at bat routine is legendary, with his toe tap, his helmet adjustment, his sliding toward the pitcher. But all hitters have a routine.

"The only thing that I do the same way every time is enter the batter's box. I've done it the same way since I was 15 years old," Baker said. "I draw three lines in the dirt. The first line I draw is where I place my back foot in the batter's box, then I draw a sweeping line across the batter's box, then I draw a third line for my front foot. The way I enter the box is as OCD as I can get. If I somehow was not allowed to enter the box the same way I always do, then I would make the effort to step out, and then make an effort to do it again."

"It's all about comfort," Baker said. "It's all about being able to do something with your eyes closed. Take Pablo Sandoval. When he gets into the box with his elaborate toe tap and the tapping of his helmet, it doesn't matter if he's in Venezuela, Cuba, Philadelphia, or Canada, it gives him a sense of peace in the box. From a physiological standpoint, in a pressure-filled situation when the crowd is really large, and the game is on the line, and you start to sweat, your heart rate will speed up significantly. But when you enter the box, and get in your comfort zone, your heart rate can do down ten to fifteen beats. It's like Nomar. His toe tap, and his adjusting his batting gloves, reminds him of his days at Georgia Tech, or in high school, when he was only playing—this wasn't work—and he wasn't under this kind of pressure. Sandoval is Nomar with a side of salsa, the Latin way, and maybe less need for a psychologist."

Clothing and Uniforms

Outfielder Torii Hunter says he has had "a thousand different superstitions, but most of them don't last very long. If I get a few hits eating peanut butter and jelly sandwiches, then I keep eating them, but when I stop hitting, I switch to . . . turkey sandwiches, or whatever."

Then he smiled and said, "But my thing has always been clean shoes. At 6:40 for every 7:05 game, I clean my shoes. I take my Mr. Bubble spray, and I scrub them until they are sparkling clean. When you look good, you feel good, when you feel good, you play good, when you play good, they pay good. If I, say, hit a double in the first inning, and I have to slide into second, now I have dirty shoes. I am so irritated. I can't wait to score now. So Miggy [Miguel Cabrera] singles me home, and as soon as I score, I run to get my Mr. Bubble, and I clean my shoes. Then I feel so much better—my shoes are sparkling clean. The clubhouse guy can clean my shoes, but no one can do it as well as I can do it myself. He might clean them, but he won't see that little spot over there. I'll see it. I'll make sure it's clean."

Shoes and socks are equally important, it seems.

"The only thing I have to have right is my socks," said catcher David Ross. "We [the Red Sox] are winning this year [2013], and I'm wearing an American flag on one sock, and the stars from the flag on the other sock. I always, always wear the stars on the right foot, but I did it wrong one day, and we lost, so I'll never make that mistake again. The stars have to be on the right foot. If we lose a game, I don't want it to be my fault for wearing the wrong socks."

Dunn said, "Socks are important. I wear NBA socks. They're thick, and low. I don't want anything tight on my calves. I hate that. Every spring, I'll get six to twelve pairs of NBA socks."

Royals DH/outfielder Jonny Gomes said, "If there's anything that comes in twos, like shoes or socks or batting gloves, I always have to put the right one on first. If I'm in an emergency situation, I wake up in the middle of the night, and without thinking, I put my left shoe on first, I will realize my mistake, and I will sit down and put my right shoe on first, then my left. When it comes to twos, the right has to come first. It has always been that way."

For some players, the entire uniform is crucial.

"Every game I pitch, I lay out my uniform the same way," said the Angels' C. J. Wilson. "I lay it out in the order in which I'm going to get dressed. So, I'll have my sleeves placed under my jersey. I'll finish it by putting my hat on top of my spikes. It's like when you were a little kid, you laid out your uniform on the foot of your bed the night before your game. This way, I am ready to go at 4 p.m. for a night game. I started doing this when I once went to the bullpen to warm up and I forgot my hat. I thought, 'What am I doing?' This is a checklist I do before every start. When I see everything is in place, I'm good."

For ex-Rays outfielder Sam Fuld, the number on the uniform is the most important part.

"Five is my favorite number," he said. "It always has been. I wore it in Little League, American Legion, everywhere. Now, I can't set my alarm clock unless it's on a five, or a multiple of five.

I can't put a microwave on any time or heat unless it is five or a multiple of it. I'm a five guy."

Baker used to be one of the catchers for closer Huston Street with San Diego.

"Huston got a bunch of saves in a row one year, maybe twenty in a row, and for the entire time, he wore the same 10-year-old sweatpants, a polo shirt, and shower shoes, the kind they give you during spring training," Baker said. "He is part owner of a clothing company, he makes $9 million a year, and he wears the same clothes three weeks in a row: something is wrong with that. But for the very superstitious, when you look at them, and they appear to be doing something that seems so wrong, then something must be going right."

Jason Motte said, "I always smell my hat. I don't know why I do that. Whenever I take my hat off, which I do all the time, I always smell my hat. Guys ask me, 'What in the world are you doing?' And I say, 'I have no idea.' But it works for me. It makes me comfortable."

And therefore, he is not changing his routine.

"I've worn the same undershirt since 2011, and I've worn the same underwear—it has holes all over it—since I got to pro ball," Storen said. "But to me, in baseball, that's normal. I wear the same necklace when I pitch. I never wear a necklace when I don't pitch. I just like the way it hits my neck when I throw. I like the way the sleeves of my undershirt grab my arms. We are all creatures of habit. The littlest things are important to us."

What about underwear?

"Some guys wear the same underwear for three weeks when they're going good, and it's noticeable—if you know what I mean—to his teammates," Baker said. "Three weeks in a row?"

"Our guy here [then-catcher] Chris Snyder looks a lot different, and prepares differently before games when he is playing," said Orioles shortstop J. J. Hardy. "Only when he is starting, he walks around in the clubhouse before the game wearing only really tight underwear, nothing else. I've run into some of his former teammates this year and they ask me, 'Hey, does Snyder still walk around in that really tight underwear when he's playing?'"

Food and Drink

The aptly named Phil Coke pointed at then-Tiger teammates Prince Fielder and Darren Downs. "See those guys," he said. "They take Oreos before every game, and each guy breaks apart an Oreo, and the one that has the most cream in it, wins. I have no idea what it means to win, I have no idea what they are doing, but they do this before every game. And to them, the breaking apart of an Oreo signifies how the game is going to go tonight."

Food and drink is crucial to a player's day, and his routine. Wade Boggs collected 3,000 hits, and made it to the Hall of Fame, eating chicken before every game. "My dad used to have me take exactly as many swings off a tee as Wade Boggs did, but I didn't eat chicken before every game. I don't like chicken," said veteran outfielder Matt Diaz. "I used to eat cold cuts. I would have a ham and turkey sandwich before every game after batting practice. Yellow mustard was preferred, though I would go with brown if I had to. And tomato. It's no wonder that I didn't lose any weight eating a hoagie before every game."

"In 2011," Storen said, "I had a grilled cheese and milk every day. Then I worried about nutrition."

Nutrition has always been extremely important to Luke Scott.

"In the morning—I mean, every morning—I have a half glass of water, a glass of orange or grapefruit juice, and some Green

Vibrance or Joint Vibrance," he said. "I don't eat for thirty minutes after that, then I have three to six eggs, Ezekial bread, and an avocado. For lunch, I will have some type of mammal flesh: deer, venison, ground or in steaks, or I'll have part of the cow that was butchered for me. Or I might have chicken or wild game. I eat at 5:30 p.m., but not a big meal, maybe some strawberries, pineapple, bell peppers, celery sticks, carrots. And I always have a protein shake during the game in the third, fourth, or fifth inning."

Wilson is equally diligent about his eating.

"I eat the same thing for breakfast before every start: a vegetable omelet with an English muffin, but it has to be a certain type of English muffin, one without butter because I'm allergic to butter," Wilson said. "I find a lactose-free English muffin, with almond butter, and a smoothie. On days I pitch, I'm not going to do anything to upset my stomach. I don't want to get a Code Brown in the third inning: the bathrooms, you know, at most major league ballparks are really, really bad. And I had a bad time in the Toronto bullpen one night. Plus, I know all the hotels on the road, I know what they have for room service, and I know all the places near the hotel that serve what I can eat that won't upset my stomach. I don't want any more Code Browns. I should be a sponsor for Pepto-Bismol."

It is a slightly different eating regimen than that of Lee Smith, who saved 478 games.

"Lee Smith, I was told, liked to sleep for the first few innings of every game," Wilson said. "I was told they'd wake him up with a cheeseburger in the fifth inning: 'Lee, time to go!'"

It's not just food, it's drink.

"In the second inning of every game, I *have to* have a cup of coffee," Diaz said. "As a bench player, I have to do it then. I don't want that first cup to come in the fifth, I don't want to be jittery if somehow I get called on to pinch-hit right after that first cup. It has to be coffee. But I've gone to the clubhouse in the second inning to get a cup, and the pot is empty. Then, I do the best I can and get a Coke. At that point, I have to lie to myself and make myself believe a Coke is coffee. It's okay to lie to myself in times of need."

Mike Dunn said, "I *have to* have a Red Bull in the first inning. When I'm in the bullpen, I always share a bag of sunflower seeds with A.J. [Ramos]. But he always has to open the bag. Always. Then I take a handful of seeds. If I don't take a handful, he nudges me, as if to say, 'You have to take a handful.' It's what we do to get us ready to pitch."

And if it's not drink, it's gum. And Elliot Johnson isn't the only one with a gum fetish.

"People think I have chew in my mouth, but it is bubble gum," said Motte. "But I don't chew it. I put two pieces of bubble gum—always plain-flavored Dubble Bubble—in my mouth before I pitch. If I go two innings, I'll change the gum after the first inning. I don't know why I do it; it worked once, so I keep doing it. I think it's the sugar. But I don't chew it. So, every time I pitch, I have chewing gum in my mouth that I don't chew.

"Pretty strange, huh?"

Hygiene

Who knew that players take a shower as often as they do?

"I take four showers a day," said Storen. "The first thing I do when I get to the park is shower."

The Nationals' Ryan Zimmerman has what ex-teammate La-Roche calls "a hit shower. He will only take a shower at the same shower. If someone else is using it, he will wait. If he's in an 0 for 10, he may have to smooth his way into that particular shower, and someone will move aside for him. There are a lot of things that guys do that they're not real proud of, but they'll do it because they think it works. That shower seems to work for Zim."

Dunn, a former teammate, said, "When Zim was in the middle of his 30-game hitting streak, I went up to him in the shower and said, 'Dude, scoot over, I need some of that water, man.' There are a lot of hits in that shower. Guys will go wherever the hits are located."

Reds second baseman Brandon Phillips said that ex-teammate catcher Ryan Hanigan "showers at the same nozzle every day when we're at home, and when we go on the road, he counts the number of nozzles until he gets to the same number that he showers at home."

Hanigan refuted that, but said, "I take two showers before every game. There are so few places where you can be alone before a game. That's why I go in the shower. That's where I go to get totally locked in for the game. But I don't want it to control my life."

It controlled Diaz's pregame routine.

"When I was in the minor leagues, I started something: I would run off the field after batting practice and take a shower," Diaz said. "Once, I ran into the shower and there were two other guys in there before the game. I just looked at them and said, 'Pregame shower guys, huh?' And they nodded. Look, I don't want to play feeling nasty. You take BP in 100 degrees in Atlanta, you get nasty. So, I have to take a shower before the game. I would rather miss a meal, I would rather play hungry, than not take a pregame shower."

Diaz laughed and said, "It's all about the mechanism. The LSU coach [Skip Bertman] used to flush the toilet after his team had a bad inning, then he'd say, 'Okay, we flushed that away. It's over. Let's go.' It's the same thing with me. Let's flush away a bad BP by taking a shower. A mechanism became a habit, which became a superstition, which became a need."

If it's not a shower, it's a hot tub.

"[Reliever] Scott Downs had a routine: he loved the contrast—he would go in the hot tub, then the cold tub," Wilson said. "Hot. Cold. Hot. Cold. 110 degrees to 45 degrees. He felt it was the best way to flush the bad stuff out of him. I couldn't do it; it was too cold. He used to pay guys like $1,000 if they could spend a minute in the cold tub. No one could."

It's all about looking good and feeling good.

"I have a thing about brushing my teeth, I'm kind of OCD about that," said Orioles first baseman Chris Davis. "I've always been that way. And I don't know why. I would never, ever forget to brush my teeth right before a game, but if I ever did, I'd be on the field, in the top of the first inning, and I would be saying to myself, 'Man, I forgot to brush my teeth!'"

Cubs manager Joe Maddon said, "I think because all the games are on TV, guys want to look good in front of the camera. A lot of guys take showers before the game, they put perfume on. They get their hair cut all the time; there's a barber in the Boston clubhouse every time we go there. I've seen guys dye their hair before a game, get their eyebrows trimmed."

And sometimes more than their eyebrows.

"I played with Todd Helton," said Cardinals outfielder Matt Holliday. "Whatever is working for him, that's what he stays with. I have seen him start a game with a full beard, and if he hasn't gotten a hit, he will go to the goatee in the fifth inning, and if he still hasn't gotten a hit, by the end of the game, he is clean shaven."

"If I have a hitting streak going, I am not getting my hair cut, there's no chance," said Elliot Johnson. "I have no idea why that is, but if I have a growth going, and I'm hitting, it stays. My longest hitting streak is 10 or 12 games. If I get to DiMaggio, I will look like a hippie."

Yet despite all the showers, cologne, and haircuts, Hunter said, "I have seen guys piss on their hands before games. It's a superstition: how in the world can that bring you good luck?"

Randy Choate

"Superstitions?" Motte said. "You *have* to talk to Randy Choate. He's messed up." Choate, 40, is a veteran situational left-handed pitcher. He is as odd as they come when it comes to superstitions and routines. He offers no explanations, and he makes no apologies.

"I do things to help rid myself of the anxiety of facing [Joey] Votto or [Jay] Bruce in a crucial situation," Choate said. "I have only been this way since I started doing the job I have now, the last five years or so. When I go to the bullpen to start to throw, I will pick up every bubble gum wrapper and every cup that might be in my sight before I start to throw. I like to have things clean around me. When I first came here, some of the guys looked at me like, 'What is wrong with you?' But now, if I just start warming up, and a loose cup blows near me, someone will pick it up and throw it away for me. I appreciate that."

Mike Dunn, Choate's teammate with the Marlins, said, "If there are pumpkin seeds on the ground when he's around, he'll go pick them all up. I've seen a napkin blow near the mound when he pitches, and he'll come off the mound, pick it up, and put it in his pocket. His work area has to be as clean as possible. We were at Citi Field recently, and the wind was blowing trash over the field. I thought to myself, 'Randy wouldn't be able to pitch right now.'"

But it's not just a clean pitching area.

"When I come to the mound, I have to pick the ball off the grass, not the dirt," Choate said. "If it's on the dirt, I have to kick it to the grass, then pick it up. If a teammate or an umpire throws me the ball when I first come in to pitch, I intentionally drop it on the grass, then I pick it up. Then I have to walk around the mound and kick the resin bag at the back of the mound. Then I throw seven warm-up pitches, only seven. I'm an even-numbered guy: I wear number 36, everything in my life is even numbers except how many warm-up pitches I throw. It's always seven, it's never eight, it's never six. Seven. Always."

There is more strangeness.

"When we throw the ball around the infield after an out, I always have to catch it from the third baseman," Choate said. "If it's the first baseman's turn to throw it to me, I will turn my back, and wait for the third baseman to throw it to me. They laugh. They tease me. But this seems to work for me. When I come into a game, if I enter from the bullpen down the left-field line, I *have* to run in between the third baseman and the shortstop. When I enter from the bullpen down the right-field line, I *have* to run between the first baseman and the second baseman. One time, [third baseman] Daniel [Descalso]—we were about seven runs ahead at the time—decided to move to a certain spot to see if I would run all the way around him on my way to the mound so I would still be running in between the shortstop and third baseman. [Cardinals manager] Mike Matheny said, 'No, stop! Stay where you are! Don't do that! We don't want to mess him up!'"

Choate smiled and said, "If I give up a hit or a walk, a mess-up in my routine is not the reason. I don't blame that for anything.

But I'm not taking any chances. I'm not the same OCD at home. I'm much more relaxed and less uptight. I just like to have everything in order."

That includes packing his equipment bag.

"I have to pack a certain way. I pack my own bag," Choate said. "They tell me, 'This is the big leagues, there's someone here to pack your bag.' I know, but I have a way to do it, everything has to go in a certain way. Sometimes, some teammates will stand there and watch me pack my bag. I ask them, 'What?' and they say, 'We just want to see the process.' I like being organized. But when I pack my bag, I always put dirty spikes on the outside of my bag, in the outside compartment. They always go in last. Always. I don't know why. I'm very clean and tidy, but I always put my spikes in last, and they have to be dirty."

Mike Dunn said, "I started to pack my own bag after watching him. My teammates came up to me and said, 'Choate, and now you? The clubbie is supposed to pack your bag.' I know, but Randy does it so well. Also, have you seen his locker? Everything is perfectly placed. When he comes to the ballpark on the road, and the clubbie has set up his locker, Randy will look at his locker and say, 'No!' and I'll sit there and watch him redo his entire locker. If the coat hangers aren't all the same—meaning not the same color, or one has a little hook inside, and the others don't—he would have it replaced: all the hangers have to be exactly the same."

But at least Choate has company in Paul Konerko.

"Come look at his locker," said Adam Dunn, a former teammate. "It's always the same. He's got his cell phone here, arranged this way. He has his watch here, and right behind it is his wedding ring. It's always the same. Sometimes I'll mess with his locker and move things around, even an inch, and he'll come back and find me and say, 'Quit messing with my locker.'"

So Dunn, just to be annoying, moved Konerko's cell phone a few inches, as well as his watch. When Konerko returned to his locker, he noticed both immediately, and quickly corrected it.

"When my locker is not right," Konerko said, "it is like, 'Aaaaaaahhhhhh.'"

He should meet Randy Choate.

Of superstitions, the Giants' Jeremy Affeldt said, "No one wears a thong anymore for good luck."

Maybe. Maybe not. Maybe we just don't know what everyone is wearing under their pants. But we do know that players believe that their routine is crucial to getting two hits tonight.

"We recently saw Miguel Cabrera, and when he got to first after taking an 0-2 pitch and just stroking it right field, I asked him, 'Teach me something, tell me how you do this,'" said La-Roche. "He said one word: 'Routine.' I told him, 'I'm going to need more than that.' He explained his tee work. Everything he does is based on his routine, which he does every day. Same thing. He kept preaching that. I always wonder if I'd be better off doing that."

David Ross said, "We are all creatures of habit. We do crazy things. When we get out of our routine, we don't know what to do. A rain delay messes everyone up, we're not sure what to do. When the off-season comes, and our routines end for the season, and I go home, I have to ask my wife, 'So, what is my role here? What am I supposed to do now?'"

Dunn said, "In the big leagues, every day is Groundhog Day. Every day is the same. It has to be. Every day, I know exactly what I'm going to be doing at 4:15. And it works for me."

Jonny Gomes said, "All these quirks that we have is to make us better players, it makes us concentrate more on what we're doing, but the irony is, it really is our way of taking our minds off the game. That's why [Atlanta's] Nick Markakis has to tap his bat on the top of his foot after every pitch. It's why [Miami's] Martin Prado writes a novel in the dirt with his bat every time he comes to the plate. Have you seen [reliever] Grant Balfour? He does something with the chain around his neck when he pitches. He is always worried where the clasp is around his neck. He adjusts it on every pitch. Watch him. One of the best closers in the game, and his clasp has to be correct. It has to be. Have you seen [Tigers DH] Victor Martinez? Every time he walks to the plate, he has one finger in his ear flap in a way like he's talking on the phone, like a CIA operative who is making a top-secret call."

Gomes smiled and said, "You can't explain this stuff. We are all screwed up. That's what the game does to us. And that's why the game is so awesome."

6. UNWRITTEN RULES

He Carries a Mariachi Band
Around the Bases

THIRTY-FIVE YEARS AGO, Wayne Gross hit a home run off reliever Ed Farmer, and took his time running around the bases. Farmer was furious and immediately plotted revenge. He didn't face Gross again until three years later, and by then, they were *teammates*. On the first pitch of a batting practice session, Farmer hit Gross in the back with a 90-mph fastball.

"What was that for!" Gross screamed.

"That was for three years ago!" Farmer screamed back.

"Okay," Gross said. "We're even!"

Welcome to the contentious, confusing, contradictory world of baseball's unwritten rules. There are many of them, and they've existed for more than a hundred years. It's hard to keep track of them, to process them, but players still live by one principle: this is a hard game played by hard men, vengeful men without remorse and with really long memories. If you disrespect them, their team, or the game, you will pay, often with something in the ribs at 90 mph.

In the 1960s, hard-throwing right-hander Stan Williams carried a list of names around in his cap. "What are the names on the list?" Williams was asked.

"Those are the guys I have to get," Williams said.

"Why do you keep them in your cap?" Williams was asked.

"So I don't forget any of them," Williams said.

The game has changed a little since those days, and some of the responsibility for the enforcement of the unwritten rules has been taken away from the people who play it: now, Major League Baseball polices the game, not the players. Now, umpires issue warnings after a questionable hit batsman, and often, the next pitcher to hit a batter gets ejected. And with the ejection often comes a suspension, sometimes for as many as 10 games.

Confusing?

"There is no fear of getting drilled anymore," said Adam Dunn, who retired after the 2014 season. "A guy in front of me, who shouldn't be celebrating when he hits a home run, does, and I'm thinking, 'Okay, they're coming after me now.' And it never comes. When you do something like that, celebrate at home plate, or make a slow trip around the bases, someone has to pay for that, preferably you. But the unwritten rules are dead. They are gone."

But make no mistake: lines that aren't spelled out in any edition of the Baseball Record Book still get crossed, and the players that cross them still face vigilante ramifications. Dunn is right, it isn't as easy to retaliate as it once was, but he overstates the situation. The unwritten rules are far from dead. They were quietly established in part to reprimand a player for running too slowly around the bases, celebrating as he goes, after a home run in the eighth inning of a 10-1 game, or, in a development of the last ten years, flipping his bat as he stands at the plate to admire his feat. The unwritten rules were built to penalize players that stole a base when ahead by 10 runs, or swung as hard as they could at a 3-0 pitch when up by 12 runs, or dropped a bunt in the ninth inning to break up a no-hitter.

And those are just a few of them.

"There are so many unwritten rules in baseball because you can't fight and you can't tackle people," said catcher John Baker. "In hockey, you throw down your gloves and fight. In football, you're allowed to tackle a guy. In baseball, there is so much separating opposing teams. You can go hard into second base, and might run over a catcher, but you can't run over the pitcher. There's not a platform for retaliation when you're frustrated or upset."

Angels pitcher C. J. Wilson said, "There are so many unwritten rules because it's such an old game. It's such a technical game. There are so many opportunities for gamesmanship. It creates such drama. It's such a game of respect. It's a game that punishes those who are selfish."

Pitcher Brandon McCarthy asks, "But aren't there unwritten rules in every industry? In journalism, you can't steal sources, right? In hockey, guys don't take their skates off and slash an opponent's throat with the blade. In football, you never see a guy take off his helmet and just bludgeon an opponent. We've been playing baseball since the 1800s. We just have more unwritten rules."

And they are all debatable and fluid and arbitrary. To some, it's an unwritten rule that a hitter shouldn't dawdle before he gets back in the batter's box. "I've yelled at hitters, 'Let's go, get in the box,'" Baker said. "But they have a certain walk-up song. They have to mimic a certain part of it, so they wait until that part of it plays. It's like they're on a runway getting into the box, instead of just playing the game." McCarthy agreed, saying, "That pisses me off, too. The rhythm of the game stops when that happens. Baseball becomes bad entertainment. The same thing applies with a pitcher that doodles around out there. That drives me just as nuts. [Boston's] Clay Buchholz is a really good pitcher, I love his stuff, but I cannot watch him because he takes so damn long between his pitches."

Wilson said, "It's ridiculous how long it takes guys to get in the box, or pitchers to throw the ball. Guys on their *own* team yell at them in very colorful language, 'Get in the box! Throw the ball!' Some guys are serial line-steppers, they are habitual line-steppers. That's how they get the reputation as a rain delay. What I love is the pitcher who has two pitches, and he shakes off the catcher five times. We yell, 'Pick one!' But really, the guy at the plate who digs a hole, adjusts his helmet, wiggles his butt, swings the bat, adjusts his wristbands? You wonder, 'What were you doing all that time in the on-deck circle?'"

A new unwritten rule was briefly established a few years ago when the Yankees' Alex Rodriguez ran across the mound after making an out, infuriating A's pitcher Dallas Braden, who claimed that the mound belongs only to the pitcher, and no runner shall cross it.

"I'm with Alex on this one," Baker said. "I'm going to have to use pretzel logic to defend Dallas, a friend. That was just Dallas showing that he grew up on the mean streets of Stockton, the whole 209 thing. He has been wildly competitive his whole life. Until that, I had never heard of it. I had never even thought about it. That was all in Dallas's mind."

Wilson said, "I always stay on the mound after a pitch, so it would be pretty awkward if a hitter ran across it while I was still standing on it. It's not a sanctimonious thing with me. Alex has had some instances where he's done some stuff, like, a few years ago, yelling at the Toronto third baseman [Howie Clark] while he was trying to catch a pop-up. That's just lame."

The Orioles' Chris Davis said, "I'd never run across the mound. I'm afraid I might trip and fall." The Marlins' Casey McGehee said, "I'd never do that. I don't want to get anywhere near the pitcher that just got me out." And Adam Dunn said, "I had never heard of it. I do it all the time. I hate to run. The fastest way to any point is a straight line."

Another unwritten rule is gaining steam: too much bling. "The guys with the eye-wash, wearing nine wristbands, and shin guards, and eye black, with seven chains around his neck," said Baker. "When you bring attention to yourself, that's when they throw at you."

And there are the million unwritten rules that govern the clubhouse. "With Arizona, we had a bathroom stall, a handicap stall, which was bigger than the rest of the stalls," said Cardinals first baseman Mark Reynolds. "There was a sign on the door of the stall that said it was only to be used by guys with four years of major league service. Really stupid stuff."

There are so many unwritten rules, Baker said, "We need to write them down." And yet if they were written down, Reynolds said, "The game would be chaos. Things happen in a game, behind the scenes, that people don't even know is going on. We keep them in house."

Chaos? Several years ago, Joe Horn, a wide receiver for the New Orleans Saints, scored a touchdown, pulled out a cell phone that he had taped inside the goalpost, and made a call.

"And no one in football cared!" Baker said. "If that had happened in baseball . . . if someone had hit a home run, reached home plate, took a cell phone out of his stirrup, and called someone, he wouldn't finish the phone call. There would be balls flying into both dugouts. It would be like a Cuban winter ball game, with guys running around with bats in their hands. Oh, my God, the world would stop spinning on its axis. The ice caps would melt."

McCarthy laughed and said, "Oh, my God, he would never get to home plate. Bats would be tomahawking out of both dugouts. Where would a player hide a cell phone, under a base?" McGehee said, "The game would never get to the next hitter. It would be so ugly."

Said veteran outfielder Torii Hunter, "That would start the greatest brawl in major league history. I would drop my glove, chase the guy down, and beat the shit out of him. And I would do the same thing if he was on *my* team. The camera shot would be of his entire team, piled on top of him, pummeling him. I hope that never happens in baseball."

Dunn said, "Oh, it's going to happen in baseball. And the guy who hits the homer will take his phone out of his back pocket and tweet it before he reaches home plate. But when that happens, I'm leaving. I'm retiring. I'm done. I'm going home."

Unwritten Rule #1: Do Not Cross the HR Pimp Line

The deliberate, demonstrative home run trot has been a part of the game for decades. The great Babe Ruth, who glamorized the home run, would wave his cap to the fans as he circled the bases. But in the last twenty-five years or so, things have gotten completely out of control. It's unclear when the real histrionics began, but Jeffrey Leonard's "one flap down" tour of the bases nearly thirty years ago was one starting point. Over the last ten years, the slow trot has been replaced, and/or preceded, by a bat flip, or a five-second pause at the plate, to celebrate the blast. As Reds flamboyant second baseman Brandon Phillips said, "If I really get one, I don't care: I'm watching. I've got to admire something."

There is a lot of admiring going on these days, a lot of bat flips and slow trots around the bases. And the score of the game or the pedigree of the home run hitter doesn't seem to matter. And sometimes, the drive they admire at home plate is caught on the warning track.

"It's the culture now, it's a young man's game," Reynolds said. "These kids grow up seeing this stuff on TV, and they want to emulate it. Baseball is a slow game, people want more action. The fans like it, the players don't like it. But more of it is going on now than ever."

Wilson said, "Look, dudes just want to get on TV. So, they pimp it at the plate. It's like the NBA. They don't want just to dunk on you, they want to say, 'He jumped all the way over that guy!' They want to see it on replay the next day. This started with Barry Bonds because he was better than anyone at hitting homers. He'd stand and fold his arms after a long home run. But I've seen guys pimp it when they are 17 years old. They're still doing it."

"I'm not a big fan of the bat flip," Davis said. "It shows up the pitcher. Sometimes, you have to act like you've been there before. The only time you should bat flip is on a walk-off."

A lot, it seems, depends on who hit the home run.

"If Manny Ramirez hits a home run, and does his thing at the plate or on the bases, well, he's Manny Ramirez, he can do that," McCarthy said. "But when Ronnie Belliard, who swings just like Manny, and does the same thing as Manny after he hits a home run, it's not the same because he's *not* Manny. I was angry for a week over that one. David Ortiz does the same bat flip after every home run. He carries a mariachi band around the bases with him every time he hits one, but it's okay because he's Big Papi. To me, it's just so arbitrary."

Orioles center fielder Adam Jones said, "If you have 50 career homers, then don't celebrate like [Robinson] Cano or Big Papi or [Alfonso] Soriano. They have 200 homers and more. It comes down to service time; when you have service time, you have certain liberties."

Royals outfielder Jonny Gomes said, "It's like the military situation: the stars on your chest and the stripes on your arms are symbols of something important, something earned: we don't wear them, we *have* them. The game gives you that, not a person, not a committee. The more you move up the ranks, the less the unwritten rules apply to you."

And yet today, the young guys are celebrating their fifth career homer as if it's number 500. The Dodgers' Yasiel Puig celebrates a meaningless double like it's a Game 7 home run.

"But I understand it," said Gomes. "You have every right to say, 'Hey, I've been waiting since I was four years old to hit a home run in the major leagues, and you want me to hurry up?' But when a young guy hits his third major league homer, and just cruises around the bases when he's up 10-0, now he has self-proclaimed stars and stripes on his shoulders."

What would Gomes tell that kid the next time he goes to the plate?

"*Duck!*" he said.

Veteran infielder Greg Dobbs said, "When you pimp a home run, or flip a bat egregiously, I'm not saying you have to put your personality in the shadows, but how far do you take it? When you do that, act selfishly, you are disrespecting the founders of the game, the guys that came before you. When you hit a homer, flip your bat, walk 10 feet toward first base and stare at the pitcher, showing bravado, you are disrespecting the other team, your team, and the name on the front of your jersey. That's the worst thing you can do."

And if a young teammate does that?

"I'd air him out," Dobbs said. "I'd tell him, 'That's not how we do things.' When you can't control yourself, you're not setting an example for children. You're not being a representative of the game, you're not representing those bigger than you. It's not about you."

McGehee said of "Cadillac-ing" it around bases in a 10-0 game, "You better not! You are going to get yourself smoked, or worse, get someone else smoked. You are an idiot, and if someone hits [Marlins star Giancarlo] Stanton, breaks his hand, and he's out three weeks, that's on you. He's hurt because you are selfish. We're here to protect people from being selfish."

Reliever Phil Coke said, "You're up 10-0, and you hit one that just goes over the outfield wall, and you're a fresh guy, you're going to get thrown at if you pimp it around the bases. I didn't see it, it happened 3,000 miles away from us, but (the Mets' Yeonis) Cespedes did that two years ago. You think, 'Hey, bro, this isn't bush league. Respect me.' You don't want to dance on Mariano Rivera's toes when you've had a cup of coffee in the big leagues. He deserves respect. He commanded respect because he showed respect."

Hunter said, "If a teammate of mine did something like that, I would light his ass up. I'd tell him, 'Don't you ever do that again!' I would tell him that because I love him, he's a teammate. And I wouldn't want him to get a bad reputation in the game, because he would."

In 2013, the then-Brewers' Carlos Gomez hit a home run off the then-Braves' Paul Maholm. Gomez says the Braves had thrown at him intentionally several times that season, so he reacted by admiring the home run, flipping the bat, making a slow run to first base, then screaming at Maholm all the way around the bases. Ten feet before he reached home plate, he was confronted by then-Braves catcher Brian McCann, which nearly started a major brawl.

The next day, Gomez apologized for his actions.

Spring 2014, Gomez said, "In the moment, it was okay to do what I did. But after I cooled down, I realized it was not the right thing. It was unprofessional of me. I've been playing this game for seven or eight years. I understand the game. I had my reasons for why I did it. But I am responsible for what I do. If a pitcher strikes you out, he can do whatever he wants to do. It makes some guys mad, but not me. If you win, you can do whatever you want.

"But this is who I am. If I try to be another way, I'm not going to be any good. I respect the game. I play hard. I have no problem with anyone from the Braves. I apologized to the Braves for my actions. I would like to apologize personally to Paul Maholm for my actions. It was my fault. It was embarrassing for me, but it was nothing personal. It was nothing personal with Brian McCann, either. If I ever get a chance to talk to him, I would tell him that. If I was a catcher, I would have done the exact same thing that he did to me."

In spring training 2014, McCann said, "I was not upset that he was pimping it around the bases. I just didn't like him yelling at our pitcher. Looking at the moment, yelling at someone like that, in any profession, it is second nature: you're going to do something about it. So I did."

Baker said, "That's the way Gomez has played his entire career. He does dumb things. I've seen him hit a homer, run about 10 feet, stop, then walk, then start to run again, like a crazy person that runs through the streets screaming at himself. It's a case of, 'Here he goes again.' But he was upset that they had hit him. I see his point. Both sides were right there."

And that is McCarthy's point. "That's where the unwritten rules work," he said. "That's what is so great about it. We can argue all day about which guy was right in that spot, Gomez or McCann."

In April 2014, Gomez was involved in a brawl between the Brewers and Pirates. He hit a deep drive to left-center field, and flipped his bat at home plate. Then, after realizing the ball would not leave the park, he ran hard to third base and wound up with a triple. Pirates pitcher Gerrit Cole, who was backing up third on the play, told Gomez that he shouldn't flip the bat unless "it's a fucking home run." Gomez yelled back, and both benches emptied, resulting in a fight and multiple suspensions, including a three-gamer for Gomez.

He didn't apologize that time, saying he did "nothing wrong." The Pirates' Travis Snider didn't apologize, either, for going after Gomez. "I was just protecting a teammate," said Snider, who was suspended for three games. That's what you do in that situation. I'd do it again." Snider got a nasty shiner in the fight courtesy of a punch from the Brewers' Martin Maldonado, who was suspended for eight games.

But apparently the unwritten rules only apply in this country. "In Japan," said McGehee, who played there last year, "it doesn't have to be a home run. When they hit a ball hard in the first inning, they flip a bat. Over there, they will flip a bat for *anything*."

Unwritten Rule 2:
There Will Be Blood . . . in Retaliation

Stan Williams might have been the only pitcher to keep a hit list in his cap, but many pitchers in baseball history would happily throw at a hitter who deserved it. "Pedro [Martinez] was notorious for that," Jones said. Reynolds said, "Oh, Randy [Johnson] would hit you." And they are two of the greatest pitchers of their generation, if not ever. When one of pitcher Rick Sutcliffe's teammates was intentionally hit by a pitch or was taken out on a cheap-shot slide at second base, or was the victim of any act that invited retaliation, Sutcliffe would walk down the bench and asked that teammate, "Who do you want me to get?"

However, it's not even clear exactly who should be "got." Should it be the player who committed the dirty, disrespectful act? Or should it be the other team's pitcher? And in the American League, with the DH, exactly how do you "get" the other team's pitcher? Should you wait to hit the best player on the other team, tit for tat? Should you only drill the guy who Cadillac-ed it around the bases? But what if he's out of the game, or is not going to bat again in that game or that series? Should you send the message immediately and just hit the next guy in the batting order?

But this is clear: they don't make them like Sutcliffe or Pedro or Randy Johnson or Stan Williams anymore. The game has changed; there aren't as many mean pitchers today as there were thirty years ago. In the mid-1990s, Art Howe, an old-school guy in many ways, managed the Astros. His team was getting pounded, opposing hitters were diving across the plate and crushing balls to the opposite field, so Howe went to one of his young pitchers.

"I need you to get the next hitter off the plate," he said.

"I can't do that," the young pitcher said.

"I'm not asking you to hit him, just get him off the plate," Howe said.

"I can't," the young pitcher said. "He and I have the same agent."

But even with the softening of today's pitchers, there are still plenty of them who are bent on revenge. "[The Tigers' Alfredo] Simon will hit you," said Reynolds. So will the Diamondbacks' Zack Greinke. Last year, he hit the Padres' Carlos Quentin with a pitch, starting a brawl that ended with Greinke having a broken collarbone. "CC will drill you," said the Orioles' Adam Jones, referring to the Yankees' CC Sabathia. "We're still pissed at the Yankees for hitting [Nick] Markakis [breaking his wrist]. We still haven't gotten them back. That was in 2012. It's 2014. And we haven't forgotten."

Some of today's pitchers forgive, but like all pitchers, they never forget.

"If they keep throwing inside to [then-teammate] Paul Gold-schmidt, then I'm coming after you," McCarthy said. "It's like little carrier pigeons taking notes back and forth on who is going to get hit next. But the line is blurred there, also, when it comes to retaliation. Is it instant retaliation? Do you do it now, or do you do it later? I've been furious at guys, and it's happened twice. But when someone admires a home run, I'm not so mad at him as I am at myself for giving up a homer."

Wilson said, "You will get drilled. Even if it takes a year, you get drilled, and you will know why. You'll say, 'Okay, that's for pimping it that day,' unless you are really ignorant, or depending on what sort of medication you are on."

Today's pitchers may be softer, but they throw harder. "No one is throwing 88 mph anymore," Dunn said. "You can only get hit by 95 so many times before you have to take action. Guys are throwing a lot harder, and with a lot more accuracy." Coke said, "A well-placed 90-mph fastball hurts like a son of a bitch."

What happens if a pitcher doesn't retaliate when the unwritten rules say he must?

"If you're paying attention, you know when someone is being thrown at," Davis said. "You are responsible for sending a message. I hope someone wouldn't have to tell a pitcher what he has to do. If you don't do it, you'll have a target on your back. You will be alienating teammates. It's not that you don't have the guts to do it, it's that you don't care."

Coke said, "It's unacceptable to not take care of business, no matter what the business is. If I'm supposed to hit a guy in the ribs, and I don't do it, then shame on me. I didn't do my job. I didn't protect my teammate. If I don't, I will never be right with the guys."

Reynolds said, "You lose respect in the clubhouse. I don't know a pitcher who wouldn't do that."

Wilson said, "One year in Tampa, one of their relievers hit Gary Matthews Jr. in the neck at about 96 [mph]. It was intentional. I was pitching in relief. It was the fourth inning of a 12-5 game. I know I have to hit someone. I know it has to be Carl Crawford because he is the equal guy. One of our veterans got in my face and screamed at me, not because he didn't think I was going to do it, he just wanted to make *sure* that I did. He said, 'You hit him in the ribs as hard as you can!' I said, 'Yes, sir.' First pitch slider, then the next pitch, I threw behind him. Crawford yelled at me. I yelled back, 'Did you not see that our guy got hit in the neck? Are you watching the game? You're lucky, I could have hit you in the face.'"

Thirty years ago, it was different. Forty, fifty years ago, someone might have got it in the face.

"Times have changed—that was much more prevalent in the '80s," Baker said. "That was more of the Wild Wild West back then. Maybe they were more serious about the game then. The pay wasn't nearly as high. They weren't as worried about losing money [over being suspended or hurt in a fight]. When George Brett slid hard into Graig Nettles at third base, that started a fistfight, and no one got thrown out. That doesn't happen anymore."

Coke said, "You don't see very often these days a pitcher say, 'I don't care, I hate you, I'm going to hit you.'"

Baker said, "In Bob Gibson's day, if you looked at him

cross-eyed, he would hit you in the head. [In 1981] Pete Rose was going for another record [the NL record for hits], he got a hit, was one hit away from the record, and Nolan Ryan told him he'd hit him in the face before he'd let him get another hit. So he struck him out the next three at bats. Things have changed. It has been cemented with the amount of money invested in these players."

Dunn said, "We've been playing the game for a hundred years. When a hitter gets drilled, his only recourse now is to take out the second baseman or the shortstop. You used to be able to run over the catcher to let the other team know that we're not going to take this anymore, but now they took that away from us. Pitchers aren't going to retaliate because they know they might be facing a suspension. We used to police this ourselves as players, but now, cameras are policing us."

Said Gomes, "So many rules and regulations have prevented the players from policing our game. Now a young guy hits a home run, he cruises around the bases, and then you hit him with a pitch to teach him a lesson, and you get suspended six games. Is it worth it to make a point? No. The rules have been altered. You have a better opportunity to go out in the parking lot and fight a guy after a game than throwing at him. If you fight in the parking lot, you might not get suspended. But if you hit a guy, you are going to get suspended."

Former Pirates catcher Russell Martin considered something much bigger and more public than a parking lot. Soon after that brawl in 2014 with the Brewers, he challenged—somewhat playfully—Maldonado to a fight in the off-season. "We would do it for charity, him against me," Martin said. "He got away with one."

And that rarely happens in baseball.

Wilson laughed and said, "The ultimate irony is that Joe Torre and Frank Robinson are legislating these things. They played against Drysdale and Gibson and Ryan. And now they're telling me that I can't make a guy's feet move, they're taking that tool away. There are guys diving out over the plate. If I can't take the inside part of the plate, I will lose my job."

McCarthy shook his head with regret. "I don't know if it's a good thing, I don't know if it's a bad thing," he said. "We romanticize so much about the past in baseball that we get into patterns about how things are supposed to be done. It is so important to keep the traditions. But the game is getting so boring to the fans. We need to keep working to change the game. And this [taking away the policing of the game by the players] is taking away from that. I miss the nasty-ass pitchers who would throw at you for just digging in or taking a big swing. There's not as much personality in the game today. The viewer has a hard time differentiating between the players, one from another. We have become so homogenized today. There should be villains in baseball. You should see a guy on TV and say, 'I really hate that guy.'"

Unwritten Rule #3:
Though Shalt Not Steal . . . up 10 Runs

In the second game of the 1984 season, the Indians, who had great speed and little else offensively, stole eight bases against the Rangers. And the Indians kept on running in the final two innings of the game, even with a four-run lead. Cleveland manager Pat Corrales responded to critics, saying, "Look, when they stop hitting home runs, we'll stop running."

It is an unwritten rule: at some point, usually when the other team's first baseman is no longer holding a runner on base, it's time to stop stealing bases. "You get a feel for how things are going in a game," Reynolds said. "You know what's going on in the heads of the other team."

The "feel" apparently wasn't being felt at Tropicana Field in a 2014 game between the Rays and Red Sox. With the Rays leading, 8-3, Yunel Escobar doubled, then took third on defensive indifference—a move that engendered a shouting match between players from the Red Sox dugout and Escobar. Gomes ran in and shoved Escobar as both benches emptied. Eventually, Gomes, Escobar, and then-Rays Sean Rodriguez were ejected. "Escobar stole third base, five runs ahead, with two outs in the seventh inning," Gomes said. "Okay. I wouldn't do that, but I don't care. But then he started screaming at our dugout, then he walked at our dugout, then he challenged our dugout. You don't do that. That's when I had a problem. I never said a word, from beginning to end. I just ran in and turned him around."

So, by how many runs must you be ahead, and how late in the game must you be, before you stop stealing?

"The unwritten rule is this: it is runs ahead against how many outs you have left," Baker said. "If you are eight runs ahead, and there are seven outs to go, you don't steal. If you are five runs ahead with two outs left, you don't steal. But, at Coors Field, a five-run lead is more like a two-run lead. In Philadelphia, a seven-run lead is a three-run lead. There has to be an adjustment for ballparks." Gomes agreed, saying, "Hey, Game 5 of the [2008] LCS at Fenway, we [Tampa Bay] are up 7-0 in the seventh inning, and we lost the game."

Joe Maddon managed that game.

"I'm not big on unwritten rules," he said. "When you're beating us by 12 runs, that's not your fault, it's our fault. If you add on two runs when you are up 12, you should. I never felt anyone was piling on. We have not played well enough. Period. Just play, baby, because at the end of the day, they didn't embarrass us, we embarrassed ourselves. It's all fluid. Some of these unwritten rules have existed since the Dead Ball Era when it took 10 singles to score four runs. They were rooted in an entirely different game. It all depends on the venue now, but to call off the jam when you are up six runs in the eighth inning, in Fenway, with Manny [Ramirez] and David Ortiz coming to the plate, that is wrong. Why stop scoring? But when they are playing behind you, and you steal, well, that's not kosher."

And what happens if you steal when you're ahead 10-0?

"Somebody is going to get drilled; it should be you, and you will deserve it," Jones said. "But you don't have to be afraid of getting it. I've been hit on purpose lots of times. It's going to happen; as long as it is not in the head or face, you're okay. There are lots of places to hit a guy: ass, elbow, back. With padding and armor, it's doesn't hurt as much. But you have to send the message."

Said Dunn, "Stealing when you're seven runs ahead in the ninth inning, you should get one right in the neck. It's stupid. It's selfish. I'm not mad at the pitcher, I am mad at *you*!"

Said Davis, "If you do, you will wear one the next at bat, next game, next year, or all three."

Said Wilson, "You don't have to steal third base when you're up 10 runs, there are lots of other ways to score. That's just a stupid chance. When you do that, you are doing something for yourself. When someone does that, the pitcher will glare at the runner. You might not get a chance to get back at them right then, you just file it away. There will be retribution."

Hunter agreed, saying, "If one of our young guys did that, I would explain it was wrong. If he does it again, that would be like puking on the floor, then licking it up. It's your fault."

Yet some base stealers, non–base stealers, and even some pitchers object to not being allowed to run, no matter the score.

"Ichiro [Suzuki] used to steal third base with two outs when he was up by five runs, even when he didn't need another bag," Jones said. "And he wouldn't get drilled, except by Texas."

"I'm scarred. I was with the Devil Rays," Gomes said. "We got behind 7-0 pretty quick all the time. At arbitration time, you'd say, 'I'd have had 20 more bags if we weren't in last place.' To me, if you are holding me on, I have the right to run."

Even a pitcher agreed.

"I don't care if the score is 24-0, if you want to steal base, go ahead," McCarthy said. "Same in football, if it's 75-0, I say throw a bomb. I don't care. Look, we all make a hell of a lot of money to get outs and to get hits. To suddenly stop trying to do those things because you are way ahead, to just stop playing after seven innings and coast to the finish line, I don't understand that logic. There are miracle comebacks in baseball. And if Billy Hamilton's team is up 25-0, he should say, 'I'm going to steal that base.' He might set the record with that one. I'm a big believer that it should be a nine-inning streak to the finish, every night, you bust your ass and do your best, the whole game."

Unwritten Rule #4: A Bunt in a No-no Is the Devil's Work

On May 26, 2001, the Padres' Ben Davis, a slow-running catcher, dropped a bunt single in the eighth inning to break up Curt Schilling's bid for a perfect game. The score was 2-0 at the time, but that bunt single set off a firestorm about when it is acceptable to bunt, if ever, during a no-hitter. Diamondbacks manager Bob Brenly called it "a chickenshit play."

"I remember that, it was awesome. I was 15 years old!" Jones said. "But you can't do that."

When—if ever—is it acceptable to bunt in a no-hitter? Most agree that it's okay to do so early in a game even if it's the first hit of the game. And most agree if the game is close late in the game, it's acceptable for a fast guy, a bunter, to lay one down in an effort to get on base. On July 31, 2011, the Angels' speedy Erick Aybar bunted on Justin Verlander in the eighth inning of a no-hitter with the score 3-0. Verlander fielded the bunt, and threw it wildly to first. The play was scored an error, but Verlander yelled at Aybar for bunting late in a no-hitter. Verlander would later lose the no-hitter, but a great debate raged in the wake of the game about Aybar's at bat.

But what about bunting in the eighth inning of a no-hitter when it's 8-0?

"That is *treason*," Hunter said.

"The unwritten rule is this: if you are just trying to break up a no-hitter, you shouldn't bunt, especially if you are someone that never bunts," Baker said. "If you are bunting to try to win the game, you should bunt. The circumstances are a big thing. If you bunt for a hit in a no-hitter when the score is 9-0, that's weak. I think 100 percent of the players would agree with that. That is not just going to get you knocked down, that is going to get you hit."

Gomes said, "If someone else did that, I would judge his character. I wouldn't fight him, I wouldn't hit him. I would look at his character. And character is really important in this game."

Wilson said, "My second year in the league, someone bunted on me when we were down 8-1. I looked at him, like 'Really?' There wasn't a no-hitter going, and that guy lost his dignity."

"That [bunting in a no-hitter] would never cross my mind," Reynolds said. "Never."

Dunn said, "It's selfish. I would never do that even if I was a bunter. He should be hit for that."

But what if the third baseman is playing way back against a power hitter?

"There's a reason I'm playing 10 feet behind third. It's because it's not within your skill set to do that, not even when the score is 2-0," Dobbs said. "So why do it when it's 8-0 in a no-hitter?"

Maddon said, "I understand the machismo that you have to earn that first hit. But I would probably encourage our guys not to bunt. If my guy had one going late with a big lead, I would take the bunt away. I would play the third baseman in. And if they did break it up with a bunt, I'd smirk or smile. I would not hit anyone. I would not say anything about it."

McCarthy might.

"I wouldn't have a problem with it, but if a non-bunter broke up my no-hitter with a bunt single in the eighth inning of an 8-0 game, I would attach the f-word to the front of his name for the rest of his career," he said. "I would refer to him for the rest of his career as Fucking John Smith."

Unwritten Rule #5: Ice a Big-lead Swing on a 3-0 Pitch

As a skinny rookie, Harold Reynolds took a big swing against veteran Nolan Ryan.

"I swung and *missed*," Reynolds said. "I didn't even hit it." The next pitch, Reynolds got one under his chin. It wasn't even a 3-0 pitch he swung at, and he still got dusted. So, if a hitter swings at a 3-0 pitch when his team is ahead 10-0?

"He is going to get killed tomorrow," Hunter said.

Not many guys are swinging 3-0 in blowouts these days. At some point, when the game appears to be over, players stop trying to swing as hard as they can at a 3-0 pitch, much like in the final seconds of a basketball game when they dribble out the final thirty seconds rather than go for another dunk.

"It's acceptable to swing at a 3-0 pitch in a 0-0 game in the fourth inning or the ninth, but you don't swing at a 3-0 pitch when it's 14-0," Baker said. "The easy way to determine the unwritten rule is this: if they're not holding runners on base anymore, you don't swing 3-0."

And if you do?

"That happened to me in the minor leagues, and I got drilled for it," McGehee said. "The guy before me did that, swung at 3-0 way ahead, and I got smoked. I went to him and said, 'Hey, if you do that again, you idiot, I will hit you. You did something stupid, and I'm paying for it.'"

Davis said, "If you swing 3-0 when you're up 10, if you do something stupid, in our clubhouse, you're going to hear it from everyone, you're going to hear it for a long time. You have to be accountable. I expect retaliation. It's not showing who is boss. This is about respect. If you do that, I'm going to take you under the stands and throw a ball at *you*."

Wilson, a pitcher, said, "When someone swings at a 3-0 up eight runs in the eighth inning, I get really competitive then. Then I *really* want to strike him out."

Coke laughed and said, "Only Miggy [teammate Miguel Cabrera] can do that [swing 3-0 whenever he likes]. He loves the game. He sees the ball, hits the ball. He's a big old donkey who just loves to swing the bat."

And yet, there is another side to this question.

"Hey, in a blowout game, you're still seeing off-speed pitches on 3-2," Gomes said. "There are no gimmies in this game. You want to take strikes away from me as a hitter? You want to take RBIs away from me? We're way ahead, so I am getting punished for that?"

McCarthy said, "If a reliever comes into a blowout game, and throws a breaking ball on 0-2, and they scream at him from the dugout to throw fastballs, why? What, do you want me to go to AAA right now? No one should stop playing and start cruising after seven innings."

ORIOLES MANAGER BUCK Showalter says the unwritten rules of the game "are being passed along by old farts like me. A lot of our young guys in the game have no idea what they mean."

The unwritten rules have been quietly and privately administered for more than a hundred years, but they are ambiguous, there are so many gray areas, and the game has changed. So, is it time to clarify them? Is it time to get rid of some of them, most of them, or do they remain essential to the game? Is the game today too public to try to exact revenge in private?

"Now everything is a humongous deal," Baker said. "There is so much more coverage now. There's *Baseball Tonight*. The game is much more transparent now on how players act."

But, McCarthy says, because the game is more transparent, it's okay for the players to become more transparent, to be more personalized, to add a little more flavor to the game. He mentioned ex-teammate Gerardo Parra, who had 17 outfield assists in 2013, and is as skilled as anyone at throwing out runners. Sometimes, when Parra guns out a guy at the plate, he will walk back to his position and subtly wag his left index finger as if to say, "Don't run on me," much like Dikembe Mutombo wagged his finger after blocking a shot.

"When Gerardo wags his finger, that is my favorite thing in the game," McCarthy said. "It's his way of saying, 'I did everything right on that play. That was a perfect play.' I love it!"

Of course, in the contradictory nature of the unwritten rules of baseball, not everyone agrees. But that's what makes the unwritten rules so interesting. How demonstrative should a player be after making a great throw? How slow is too slow a trot around the bases? When should a pitcher retaliate against a hitter, and how? What should the score be before you stop trying to steal a base, or stop swinging on a 3-0 count? When can you bunt in a no-hitter?

Even after more than a hundred years of baseball, there are no definitive answers to these questions, and there likely won't be over the next hundred years. But Dunn, who retired after the 2014 season and a fourteen-year career, has had enough of the ambiguity of the unwritten rules, which he says are dead and gone. He says it is time for change. And he has a solution.

"To me," he said, "it should be mandatory: you can drill one guy per game, and you can have one charge of the mound per game. Fair is fair."

7. SACRIFICE FLIES

A Standing Ovation for an F-7

THE CARDINALS' MATT Carpenter came to the plate with the bases loaded and one out in the fifth inning at Wrigley Field on August 17, 2013. He hit a high pop-up to the shortstop. The infield fly rule was called. After Cubs shortstop Starlin Castro had caught the ball, he wandered around, not paying attention, so the runner on third base, Jon Jay, tagged up, and scored. So, Carpenter hit a 110-foot infield pop-up on which he was automatically called out because of the infield fly rule, but Carpenter wound up with an RBI and no official time at bat because that pop-up to the shortstop was correctly scored a sacrifice fly.

And you wonder why I'm fascinated by sacrifice flies.

I am referring to the ridiculous statement I made on *Baseball Tonight* on July 1, 2007—"I'm fascinated by sacrifice flies"—after the Astros' Carlos Lee had hit his 13th of the season, setting the club record before he got to the All-Star break, and seemed destined to break the MLB record of 19 sacrifice flies in one season. Since that broadcast of *Baseball Tonight*, friends and colleagues, as well as Cardinals pitcher Adam Wainwright, have not let me forget it. If a game involves sacrifice flies in an unusual way, someone mentions it to me, as if I am the official keeper of such things, which I am not. But on June 11, 2014, the Royals beat the Indians 4-1. The Royals scored all four runs on sacrifice flies, the first team to score all four runs in one game, on sacrifice flies since the 1980 Expos, and the first team ever to *win* a game-scoring all four runs on, sacrifice flies. A few days later, Wainwright, ever playful and hilarious, asked me, "Is that your greatest game of all time?"

No, it is not, and yet I must defend my stance on sacrifice flies. I must explain that they are not meaningless, humorless, pointless. They are very interesting, and yes, even fascinating.

You don't even have to hit a ball in fair territory to get credit for a sacrifice fly: if a foul fly ball is caught in the outfield and the runner tags up and scores, that's a sacrifice fly. Really, in what other play in baseball can you not hit a ball fair, and still wind up with an RBI?

You can get a sacrifice fly while hitting into a double play: runners at first and third, the runner on third scores on a fly ball, the runner on first is thrown out trying to advance, but if the runner on third scored before the third out was made at second, the run counts, and that's a sac fly.

You can reach base and be credited with a sacrifice fly: runner on third base, fly ball to deep left, left fielder drops the ball, the runner on third, who was tagging up, scores. The batter gets credit for a sacrifice fly if the official scorer rules that if the left fielder had caught the ball, the runner would have scored. So, it's an RBI, no time at bat, sac fly, batter reaches on an error.

There doesn't even have to be a man on third base to get a sacrifice fly. In 2014, then Rays Matt Joyce hit a fly ball that went so deep to center, Desmond Jennings tagged up and scored from second base. You can get two RBIs on one play without getting

an at bat if you fly out and the outfielder's throw is errant, allow-
ing the runners on second and third to tag up and score. Mike
Trout got two such RBIs in 2012, the first Angel to do that since
Rupe Jones in 1986.

According to the Elias Sports Bureau, sacrifice flies were recognized as an official statistic from 1908 till 1930, then again in
1939, but not continuously until 1954, which perhaps explains why
the best and most famous baseball broadcaster ever, Vin Scully,
still refers to them as "scoring fly balls," not sacrifice flies, because
sacrifice flies weren't a statistic when he started doing Dodger
games in 1950. From 1926 to 1930, sacrifice flies were credited for
advancing a runner to any base with a fly ball. But for the purposes
of this chapter, we are only recognizing sacrifice flies after 1953.

There are so many arcane, obtuse, complicated statistics involving sacrifice flies. Here are a just a few of them.

⊕ In 1954, Dodger Gil Hodges had 19 sac flies, which remains the record. How strange is that?

⊕ Eddie Murray is the all-time record holder with 128, yet he
never led his league in sacrifice flies in any season. How
can that be? Following Murray's 128 are 127 by teammate
Cal Ripken. Another Oriole, Brooks Robinson, holds
the record for the most seasons leading or tied for the
league lead in sacrifice flies with four. Johnny Bench, Ron
Santo, and Dante Bichette led their league three times.
Murray, a Hall of Famer, never led or tied for his league
lead in sacrifice flies in a season, yet the following obscure
players did: Leo Posada, Barry Foote, Jack Heidemann,
Rick Wilkins, Clay Dalrymple, and Alan Bannister, who
tied with Carl Yastrzemski for the American League

lead in 1977. Heidemann tied for the AL lead with Rico Petrocelli with 10 in 1970, but finished his career with only 15 sacrifice flies. Posada tied with Minnie Minoso and Vic Power for the AL lead in 1961 with 12. They were the only 12 Posada hit in his three-year career.

① Ten times starting in 1954 a player has hit three sacrifice flies in one game, the last being José López in 2008. And then there is Adam Dunn. In 2004–05, he went 1,085 plate appearances without a sacrifice fly. He had 65 opportunities to hit one—runner at third base, less than two out—before he finally broke his streak with a routine fly out to left field. The crowd at Great American Ballpark cheered him heartily. Dunn raised his arms in triumph. Years later, with a big smile, Dunn said, "I have to be the only player in major league history to get a standing ovation for hitting a routine fly out to the left fielder."

① Chili Davis drove in 112 runs in 1993, the record for RBIs in a season without a sacrifice fly. One of Davis's former teammates, Eduardo Pérez, said that Davis told him that he never went to the plate thinking about hitting a sacrifice fly. He said it wasn't the correct mentality for a hitter to go to the plate thinking he was going to make an out. Plus, he said, if he tried to hit a fly ball, he might end up hitting an easy pop-up to an infielder. And yet, Davis hit 94 sacrifice flies, a lot for a guy that never intended to hit one. In 1988, he tied Ripken (the only season in which Ripken led his league) for the AL lead with 10.

① Dunn (102-0 for the 2004 Reds) and Nick Esasky (108-0 for the 1989 Red Sox) are the only other players since 1953 to drive in 100 runs in a season without hitting a sacrifice fly. Compare that to Heidemann's 1970 season. He drove in only 37 runs—but 10 on sacrifice flies, meaning more than one-quarter of his RBIs came in at bats in which he didn't even get a hit.

① Bob Boone, a career .254 hitter with 105 home runs, had as many or more sacrifice flies in his career (78) than Willie McCovey, Harmon Killebrew, Mark McGwire, Reggie Jackson, Sammy Sosa, and Mickey Mantle, all of whom hit 500 home runs. Mantle hit 47, as many as Mickey Tettleton, and only one more than dinky little infielder Neifi Perez. Neifi Perez? Maybe this is explainable, because those 500–home run guys were also swing-and-miss guys, as is Dunn. Boone was a contact guy who was one of the best at putting the ball in play. And, maybe, once those 500–home run hitters got the ball up in the air, it didn't end with a sacrifice fly, it usually ended up as a home run.

① In 1991, the Mets' Howard Johnson tied the National League record for most sacrifice flies in a season by a switch-hitter with 15, a statistic about which Steve Hirdt of the Elias Sports Bureau wrote in the annual *Elias Baseball Analyst*, "My God, we've created a monster!"

① Nolan Ryan is the all-time leader in sacrifice flies allowed by a pitcher, with 146. The record for most sacrifice flies allowed in a season is 17, by Larry Gura (1983) and Jaime Navarro (1993).

① Charlie Hough, a knuckleball pitcher, holds the record for most times (four) leading his league in sacrifice flies allowed.

And yet another knuckleballer, Phil Niekro, threw 284⅓ innings in 1969 without giving up a sacrifice fly.

① Bob Gibson, a pitcher, hit 18 sacrifice flies in his career, one more than outfielder Mark Whiten, who once hit four home runs in one game.

① The record for most at bats in a season without hitting a sacrifice fly is held by Pete Rose (1973, his MVP season), Frank Taveras (1979), and Kirby Puckett (1986), and each had exactly 680 at bats in those years. How odd is that?

① The record for most career plate appearances without a sacrifice fly is 858 by Cody Ransom. Trust me, I have and will continue to check every day to see if he gets his first one.

① And finally, only two players have led the major leagues in consecutive seasons in sacrifice flies: Bengie Molina (2008–09)—Bengie Molina?—and our guy, Carlos Lee (2007–08).

But here is the kicker to this whole, completely preposterous story. Lee hit his 13th sacrifice fly of the season that night, July 1, 2007, and seemed well on his way to breaking Gil Hodges's record for sacrifice flies in a season. And yet, Lee didn't hit another sacrifice fly the rest of that season.

Now *that* is fascinating.

8. BONDS HR NAMES

Desperately Waiting for Barney-Fife

I LOVE BASEBALL names. I always have. It has always intrigued me that the first name in the *Baseball Encyclopedia*, which lists players alphabetically, hitters first, then pitchers, is Hank Aaron, one of the game's greatest, and for years, the all-time leader in homers and RBIs.

When I was young and had no other interests in life, I compiled the All-Currency Team (Norm Cash, Ernie Banks, Don Money, etc.), the All-Animal Team (Doug Bird, Nellie Fox, and Felix "The Cat" Mantilla, etc.), and the All-Presidents Team (pitcher Grant Jackson was the captain, for obvious reasons). Now that I'm old and have no other interests in life, I still love to look at baseball names to see what peculiar combinations they might bring.

Every day, I look at the starting batteries—pitcher and catcher—in hopes that one will provide something different and fun. Abbott and Castillo—Glenn Abbott pitched and Marty Castillo caught for the Tigers—was a favorite until the best battery of all time came along. Bud Black pitched and Steve Decker caught for the Giants—Black and Decker—which prompted my genius friend

Steve Rushin to write that, on those days, Decker would wear "the power tools of ignorance." Others have included Royals pitcher Dan Quisenberry and catcher Jamie Quirk—Q to Q; and in 2013, Guillermo Quiroz caught the Giants' Barry Zito, marking the first Z-Q, or Q-Z battery since Todd Zeile caught Quisenberry in 1989. But alas, I don't understand how baseball, which never lets us down, could not have allowed us the pleasure of Barry Foote catching Bill Hands or Rich Hand.

I always check the day's starting pitchers just in case some pattern forms. On July 4, 2012, the day we celebrate our independence, the following pitchers threw the first pitch of the game: Kennedy, Lincoln, Jackson, two Johnsons, Adams, and Madison Bumgarner. Starting pitcher matchups are something I check daily, also. The Mason-Dixon matchup with Mike Mason and Ken Dixon happened more than once in the 1980s, and in more recent years, we had a Minor-Leake, Diamond-Sale, Cole-Hahn, Lee-Strasburg, Kennedy-Oswalt, and Niemann-Marcum as well as an all-time favorite when Gavin Floyd started against Brian Bannister, giving us a Floyd-Bannister matchup, which was so great because Bannister's father is Floyd Bannister, who pitched for many years for the White Sox. And I forever hope that Stolmy Pimentel, formerly of the Pirates, returns to the major leagues and pitches in a game against the Mets' Matt Harvey, so the headline can read: "It Was a Dark and Stolmy Night— Harvey, of course, being known as the Dark Knight."

The Blue Jays used to have David Bush and Brandon League in their bullpen, and several times Bush replaced League or League replaced Bush for the famous Bush-League bullpen. In 2011, the Rockies brought Matt Lindstrom out of the bullpen, then followed him with Matt Reynolds, then followed him with Matt Belisle: three Matts in a row. Also in 2011, the Astros used Wandy Rodriguez, Fernando Rodriguez, and Aneury Rodriguez, marking the first time since 1900 that three pitchers with the same surname pitched in the same game. In 2012, the only two position players in the game's history named Dustin, Boston's Pedroia and Seattle's Ackley, were the second basemen in the same game. Before 2000, there were no major league players ever with a first name Brandon, but twelve to thirteen years later, the A's had four on their roster, three of them first basemen: Brandon Moss, Allen, and Hicks.

Double-play partners make for good combinations, none better than when the Phillies in the 1960s had shortstop Bobby Wine and second baseman Cookie Rojas, a period known as the Days of Wine and Rojas. Batter-pitcher matchups can be good, few better than pitcher Joe Niekro against Phil Niekro: Joe hit one career home run, and it came off his brother. But I am still wondering how, in 2013, that Cubs manager Dale Sveum could have given second baseman Darwin Barney the day off against the Dodgers' Stephen Fife, preventing the first Barney-Fife at bat in major league history. And I will consider retiring, because there will be nothing worth sticking around for, when Rockies reliever Rex Brothers faces Melvin and Justin Upton in the same game, for a Brothers against the brothers.

In 2014, the Giants formed a lineup in which seven of their starters had five letters in their last name, and the Cardinals got a home run from three players named Matt in the same game. Nothing was better than in 2014, when for the first time in history, MLB team—the Mets— had three players with a last name that began with a lower case "d": catcher Travis d'Arnaud, outfielder Matt den Dekker, and pitcher Jacob deGrom. The equipment man for the Mets only had one lower case "d," so for two of the guys, he used an upside down "p."

All of which brings us to Barry Bonds. When he became the all-time home run hitter, or at least hit more home runs than anyone else in history, I looked at all the pitchers off whom he hit a home run, thinking there must be some interesting combinations there. Here's what I found.

Barry Bonds hit a home run off 449 different major league pitchers, from Kyle Abbott to Barry Zito. He played no favorites; he homered off all colors, professions, in all weather, in all places, off all sizes, off famous people, off royalty, off Padres, off brothers, and off ESPN.

He homered off Abbott and Castillo, Dustin and Hoffman, Murphy and Brown, Ebert and Roper, Clay and Fraser, Green and Bere, Charles and Darwin, Franklin and Marshall, Price and Wright, Reed and Wright, Frey and Cook, Long and Foster, Mays and Aaron Heilman. He homered off a Grahe, Black, Brown, Greene, Mark Redman, and Wally Whitehurst. He homered off Sun-Woo Kim, Steve Rain, and David Weathers. He homered off a Gardner, a Painter, a Carpenter, a Brewer, a Weaver, a Cook, a Hunter, a Priest, and a Doc.

He homered off Mr. Haney, Mr. Howell, and Mr. Tibbs. He homered off a King, a Duke, and Jason Marquis. He homered off early American history: Franklin, Adams, Hamilton, and Henry. He homered off a Person, a Wolf, and a Byrd. He homered off Mike Myers, Kenny Rogers, and Hitchcock. He homered off a Park, a Beech, and Parris. He hit a shot off Winchester and a drive off Mulholland.

He homered against six sets of brothers. He homered off five Smiths and the Family Robinson: Jeff D., Ron, Don, and Robinson Checo. He homered off 6'11" Eric Hillman and 5'9" Steve Frey. He homered off Loewer, Leiter, and in Jeff Juden, heavier. He homered off the aptly named Ted Power, Bill Long, Kelly Downs, Pat Rapp, and Jack Armstrong.

So, three cheers for Bonds, who homered off a Woody, a Cliff, and a Fraser, which was his Norm.

9. THE QUIRKJIANS

*Thrown Out by All Three Molinas
in 12 Days*

SECOND BASEMAN IAN Kinsler is the son of a former prison warden. "We had some interesting discussions at the dinner table," he said.

Pitcher Phil Coke is the son of a former prison guard. "Some of the stories he told," Coke said, "I was like, 'Are you shittin' me?'" For years, I waited and waited for them to face each other in a regular season game. It would have been the greatest at bat ever, but much to my dismay, it never happened. In 2014, they became teammates on the Tigers, and at least they took part in a few plays, the first being a 1 to 4 putout. On *Baseball Tonight*, I called it "The *Shawshank Redemption* Force-out," and followed it with the worst Morgan Freeman impersonation ever.

Kinsler-Coke is a Quirkjian. A Quirkjian is something quirky, some statistical oddity or something peculiar in the playing of the game or something that joins players from a hundred years apart in pairings and lists that make no sense. Some Quirkjians, such as Kinsler-Coke-*Shawshank*, are stupid and pointless, but that's what makes baseball so much fun; baseball has always been built for the strange, stupid, and senseless stuff.

Quirkjians are my favorite things to find. They enhance my viewing of any game, my daily memorization of the box scores, and my tremendous love for the history of the game. Some are easy to find; some take tremendous time and research. When pitchers hit, and non-pitchers pitch, Quirkjians generally follow. Wild games, long 0-fers, big innings, terrible pitching performances, cycles, and odd-size players facing or replacing odd-size players always make for good Quirkjians. When a big number just sort of appears in a box score, such as a 5 in a batter's strike-out line, or Manny Parra's bizarre 2007 pitching line—3-3-3-3-3-3—making him the first starting pitcher to have all 3s since Sonny Siebert in 1975, that's usually a Quirkjian. And when in need, always look to Adam Dunn, who for fourteen years was a walking, talking Quirkjian with all his strikeouts, walks, long home runs, and funny remarks. In 2014, after going through every batting line of Dunn's career, I found the only game in which he had four official at bats, had three hits—all singles—and didn't strike out. I can't begin to tell you how sad and depressed I am that he retired after the 2014 season.

With Dunn, and with any Quirkjian, the key is being curious enough to ask, "When was the last time that happened?" or "How odd is that?" Then I try to find the answer, but if I can't without help, my first call goes to my friends at the Elias Sports Bureau, the official scorekeeper for the four major sports. The things they can find, often in a matter of minutes, are incredible. My favorite words from the Elias are "For the first time since 1900 . . ." or "He is the first player ever . . ." Which means: there have been more than 200,000 major league games, and the game last night, or the play or the box score line, had never happened in well over a hundred years of games, plays, and box score lines. And we just saw it. I love that.

Here are the best of the Quirkjians, 2008–14.

Best of 2014

Neil Walker became the second player ever to hit a walk-off home run in a 1-0 victory on Opening Day, joining another Pirate, Bob Bailey, who did so off Juan Marichal in 1965.

Walker also joined Minnie Minoso, Sixto Lezcano, Jim Presley, and Tony Batista as the only players ever to hit a walk-off homer and a grand slam on Opening Day in their careers.

Tigers shortstop Danny Worth, using a knuckleball, became the first non-pitcher since 1969 to throw one scoreless inning in a game with two strikeouts.

Mets pitcher Bartolo Colon joined Diomedes Olivo of the 1962 Pirates as the only players ever to record their first career extra-base hit as a 40-year-old.

The Mets' Wilmer Flores became the first player in history to drive in six runs in a game as a second baseman and six runs in a game as a shortstop in the same season.

The Tigers and Yankees played twelve innings with no walks, the first time that has happened in a game that long since the Dodgers beat the Pirates in thirteen innings in 1917.

Cubs catcher John Baker pitched the sixteenth inning, got the victory, and scored the winning run. He became the first player to record his first major league victory and score the winning run since Ryan Hancock, a pitcher for the Angels, on June 9, 1996.

Best of 2013

The Dodgers' Clayton Kershaw became the second starting pitcher ever to hit a home run to break up a scoreless tie in the eighth inning or later, joining Juan Pizarro, who homered off Tom Seaver in 1971.

The Dodgers' Matt Magill became the first pitcher ever to walk nine and allow four homers in one game, which means he had more walks and almost as many homers allowed in six innings as Dennis Eckersley had in 131 innings in the 1989–90 seasons.

The Phillies' John Mayberry Jr. became the first player ever to hit two home runs in extra innings of the same game, the second one being a walk-off grand slam.

The Rockies' Carlos Gonzalez hit three homers, and Troy Tulowitzki went 5 for 5 with two homers, the first time in major league history that teammates have done that in the same game.

The A's Adam Rosales joined Graig Nettles in 1969 as the only players in the last hundred years to strike out four times in extra innings having not played in the first nine innings.

Josh Hamilton joined Jeff King in 1990 as the only players since 1939 to ground into three double plays and strike out twice in the same game.

The Rangers became the second team in history to win all three games of a series with a walk-off home run, meaning they had more walk-off home runs in three games than the Mariners had in the last four seasons.

Best of 2012

The Rangers' Adrian Beltre joined Joe DiMaggio in 1948 as the only players to hit for the cycle and have a three-homer game in a seven-day period.

The Orioles' Chris Davis hit three home runs in one game, joining Babe Ruth in 1930 and Jim Tobin in 1942 as the only players since 1900 to have a three-homer game and a victory as a pitcher in the same season. Tobin did both in the same game, the only pitcher ever to hit three homers in one game.

The Royals became the second team ever, joining the 1931 Yankees, to score six runs in the first inning, and none in the next eight.

The Marlins became the first team since the Browns in 1914 to steal seven bases in a game in which they only scored one run. Braves pitcher Tommy Hanson became the first pitcher since Bob Feller in 1936 to have seven walks, seven strikeouts, and seven stolen bases allowed in one game.

The Twins' Francisco Liriano became the first Twin ever to strike out 15 in a game and lose, and became the only pitcher since 1900 to strike out 15 and allow a grand slam in the same game.

Aaron Hill hit for the cycle for the second time in 12 days. Only three teams have ever had a player hit for the cycle twice in a calendar month. And, in 12 days, Hill had one more cycle than the Rays, Padres, and Marlins had in their franchise histories combined.

The Mariners became the fourth team since 1900 to score eight runs in consecutive innings. They sent thirty men to the plate and scored 16 runs before Texas' number 8 hitter, Mitch Moreland, came to the plate.

The Mets' Jeremy Hefner recorded his first major league victory, and hit his first major league home run, in the same game. Hoyt Wilhelm did that, as did Jim Palmer, but the last pitcher to do it was Dennis Tankersley in 2002. He never hit another homer and never won another game.

The Marlins did something that no team had done since 1900: four different Marlins pitchers—Josh Johnson, Randy Choate, Steve Cishek, and Mike Dunn—walked four straight batters against the Mets.

Mets reliever Jon Rauch, who is 6'11", faced Astros second

baseman Jose Altuve, who is 5'5", which is believed to be the greatest disparity in height between a pitcher and a batter in baseball history.

The Astros used seven different pitchers to face seven consecutive Mets batters. That had never happened in baseball history.

The Red Sox's Adrian Gonzalez drove in the only run in a 1-0 victory, the only time he had done that in his career. Alex Rodriguez had never done that. Ted Williams did that nine times; Brooks Robinson did it ten times.

Brandon Inge had three 4-RBI games in a four-game span; Lou Gehrig is the only other player in baseball history that has done that.

The Orioles became the first team in American League history to hit homers back-to-back-to-back to start the first inning—by Ryan Flaherty, J. J. Hardy, and Nick Markakis. The last time a team did that was the 2007 Brewers. Hardy was the second homer hitter in that game, also.

Twins catcher Drew Butera pitched against the Brewers. He and his dad, Sal, became the first father-son combination of non-pitchers ever to pitch in a major league game.

In Brewer catcher Jonathan Lucroy's first game ever as a cleanup hitter, he drove in seven runs. The last player to drive in that many runs in his first game as a cleanup hitter was Tommy McCraw, who had eight in a game in 1967.

Best of 2011

The Royals' Vin Mazzaro became the only pitcher in history to allow 14 runs in fewer than three innings in one game. So, in 2⅓ innings, Mazzaro allowed as many runs as Bob Gibson allowed from June 2 to September 2, 1968, a stretch of 19 starts, and 165 innings.

Craig Counsell had an 0-for-45 streak, which tied Bill Bergen in 1909 and Dave Campbell in 1973 for the longest streak by a position player since 1900. In between hits by Counsell, the Red Sox's Dustin Pedroia had 75 hits.

Jake Westbrook hit a grand slam to make the Cardinals the only team in history to get a grand slam from a pitcher three years in a row. The team that allowed it, the Brewers, became the first team ever to allow a grand slam to a pitcher and get a grand slam from a pitcher—Shawn Marcum—in the same season.

The Mets went 299 games without a grand slam, allowing 18 in that time, then hit slams in consecutive innings. Brooklyn in 1901 was the last team to go at least 250 games without a slam, then hit two in a game. Daniel Schlereth gave up both slams against the Mets, meaning he gave up two more slams in two innings than Jim Palmer allowed in 3,948 innings.

We saw something we've never seen: a fielder's choice, error right fielder. Mets pitcher R. A. Dickey, who was on first base, got confused on whether Justin Turner's one-hop line drive to right field would be caught. Dickey was hung up between first and second when Phillies right fielder Domonic Brown bobbled the ball, allowing Dickey to go to second. Brown received an error, with no hit for Turner.

The first seven Brewers that batted in the eleventh inning did not have an official plate appearance: walk, sacrifice, sacrifice fly, hit by pitch, walk, sacrifice fly, walk. It was the first time that had happened since July 25, 2003, and the shortstop and third baseman on defense in both games were Jimmy Rollins and Placido Polanco.

The Braves' Brian McCann joined Jeff Heath in 1949 as the

only players ever to hit a game-tying, pinch-hit home run in the ninth inning, and a walk-off home run in extra innings.

Best of 2010

Mets reliever Ryota Igarashi turned 31, and became the twelfth pitcher ever to allow a walk-off home run on his birthday. The last was Lance Painter in 2003.

Umpire Bob Davidson ejected Tampa Bay's Carl Crawford and Joe Maddon to pass Joe West for most ejections—133— among active umpires. The next day, Joe West ejected the White Sox's Mark Buehrle and Ozzie Guillen to retake the lead with 134.

Edwin Jackson threw one of the strangest no-hitters in history. He faced 40 batters, tying for most in a no-hitter since 1900. He threw 79 strikes, 70 balls—the most balls thrown by any pitcher since 2000. He walked eight, two short of Jim Maloney's major league record for walks in a no-hitter. And Jason Bartlett became one of eight players ever to make the final out of two no-hitters, joining, among others, Hank Aaron and Ted Williams.

When Omar Infante and Jason Heyward hit two home runs each in the same game, it marked the first time since 1900 that the 1-2 hitters for a team each homered twice in the same game.

The Cardinals and Mets played twenty innings. It marked the first time two non-pitchers pitched in the same game since the 1990 Expos, and the first time two pitchers pitched in a non-blowout game since 1945. It marked the first game that was scoreless through eighteen innings since 1989. It was the first game ever that was scoreless through eighteen, and didn't end in a shutout. The Mets became the third team ever to play twenty innings, not get an extra base hit, and win.

Best of 2009

Nationals pitcher Daniel Cabrera finally put a ball in play after striking out for the first 17 at bats of his career. He grounded out to first base against Chris Volstad. On his next at bat, he reached base on a walk from Hayden Penn.

The Marlins' Hanley Ramirez became the first shortstop to drive in five runs on Opening Day since the Phillies' Don Money in 1969. Khalil Greene became the first Cardinal shortstop to hit cleanup on Opening Day since Rogers Hornsby in 1919. And Rangers shortstop Elvis Andrus became the first player named Elvis to hit a major league home run, meaning it was the first time we could truly say that Elvis has left the building.

Yankee first baseman Nick Swisher pitched. He became the first non-pitcher since Cubs outfielder Willie Smith in 1968 to hit a home run, throw a scoreless inning, and strike out a batter in the same game.

Aaron Laffey became the first pitcher since Les Cain in 1970 to throw a double-play grounder in five straight innings. So, in five innings, Laffey threw more double-play ground balls than Don Sutton threw in 254 innings in 1975.

Gary Sheffield became the fifth Met to hit a triple as a 40-year-old. The other four are—get a load of this—Willie Mays, Moises Alou, Orlando Hernandez, and Frank Tanana. The last two are, of course, pitchers. Those were the only triples that they hit in their careers.

Tigers manager Jim Leyland said he'd never seen it before . . .

that's because almost no one had seen it before. The Yankees became the second team in history—and the first American League team—to break up a scoreless tie in the seventh inning by scoring 10 runs in an inning.

Marlins outfielder Cody Ross pitched in a game to become only the second player ever named Cody to pitch in a major league game. The first was Cody McKay, who also was not a pitcher—he was a catcher—but in a blowout game was called on to pitch.

Red Sox center fielder Jacoby Ellsbury tied a major league record with 12 outfield putouts. In the same game, Blue Jays center fielder Vernon Wells had none.

The Mets' Livan Hernandez got consecutive outs in the seventh inning without throwing a pitch. He picked the Cardinals' Joe Thurston off second, then, before another pitch was thrown, Albert Pujols took off for second. Hernandez stepped off the mound and threw him out at second.

Red Sox right fielder J. D. Drew completed the rare 9-2 force-out, scooping up a line drive by Ryan Freel and throwing out Miguel Olivo at the plate.

Mark Buehrle's perfect game was caught by Ramon Castro, the first perfect game ever in which the catcher caught the pitcher for the first time.

Manny Ramirez hit the first pinch-hit home run of his career. That's all the pinch-hit homers Babe Ruth had in his career, and it's one fewer than Mike Schmidt and Frank Robinson.

When Jason Marquis took over the major league lead with his 12th victory, he became the first Rockie ever to lead the major leagues in victories at any point after the first day of any season.

In Oakland's 14-13 victory over the Twins, the A's won a game that they were 10 runs down for the first time since 1925. The A's became the first team since 1941 to win a game in which their starting pitcher—Gio Gonzalez—allowed 11 earned runs. Justin Morneau became the first Twin ever to hit two home runs and drive in seven runs in a loss.

Phillies catcher Paul Bako hit a home run for his eighth different team, as many as Gary Sheffield and Bobby Bonds. But Bako had only 22 career homers, fewest for anyone to homer for eight teams.

When Jayson Werth hit a grand slam, scoring Ryan Howard, Chase Utley, and Raul Ibañez, it marked the first time in baseball history that a player with 30 home runs hit a home run that scored three other players who had 30 home runs that season.

Chris Carpenter joined Blue Moon Odom, Micah Owings, and Robert Person as the only pitchers since the start of divisional play in 1969 to drive in six runs in a game. Carpenter did so in only five innings, joining Person and Vic Raschi in 1953 as the only pitchers in baseball history to have more RBIs than innings pitched in a game.

Best of 2008

Ryan Zimmerman hit a walk-off home run in the first game played at Nationals Park. He became the third player in history to christen a new ballpark with a walk-off homer, joining Bill Bruton at County Stadium in 1953, and Dante Bichette at Coors Field in 1995.

Ken Griffey Jr. hit his eighth Opening Day home run, passing Babe Ruth and Willie Mays and tying Frank Robinson for the most in history. Johnny Bench, with 389 home runs, has the most career home runs without a home run on Opening Day.

Frank Thomas set a major league record for most at bats—9,832—without a sacrifice bunt. He said he never had one in

Little League, high school, college, or the minor leagues. He said his only attempt in the major leagues was early in his rookie year. He fouled off the first pitch, then hit away.

Toronto's Jesse Carlson became the first pitcher since Jack Sanford in 1960 to enter a game with the bases loaded, then strike out the side.

The Phillies scored 20 runs in a game for the second time this year. The last time the Phillies scored 20 runs twice in one season was 1900. In the decade of the 1960s, teams scored 20 runs in a game six times. The Phillies did it twice in three weeks.

For the first time in the history of Coors Field, there was a scoreless tie through eight innings. That ended a streak of 1,075 games at Coors with at least one run being scored in the first eight innings, the longest in any ballpark in the history of baseball.

In the 726th regular season appearance of his career, Greg Maddux had a first: it was the first time he'd ever hit a batter, thrown a wild pitch, and made a fielding error in the same game.

Prince Fielder hit the second inside-the-park home run of his career, which means he had twice the regular season totals of Rickey Henderson and Ichiro Suzuki combined.

On June 22, the Rangers' Ian Kinsler and the Nationals' Willie Harris became the first players in history to hit a home run on their birthday in the same game.

Trevor Hoffman allowed his 87th career home run, most in NL history by a pitcher who has never started a game.

In a twelve-day period, Jose Reyes was thrown out for stealing by all three Molina brothers. On June 27, Jose Molina got him. On July 1, Yadier got him. And on July 8, Bengie threw him out.

The Rangers' Ian Kinsler extended his hitting streak to 23 games. He and Michael Young became the first second baseman/shortstop combination to each have a 20-game hitting streak in the same season since 1900.

In the All-Star Game, Dan Uggla made three errors, struck out three times, and grounded into a double play. Not only was that a first in All-Star Game history, but he's the first player in any major league game to do that since "grounded into double plays" became official in 1933.

CC Sabathia became the third pitcher in history to hit a home run in both leagues in the same season. He joined Earl Wilson in 1970 and Jim Tobin in 1945.

The Rangers' Ramon Vazquez had the walk-off hit in a game in which he made three errors, making him the first player since Bob Brenly in 1986 to do that. Brenly made four errors in that game, but ended it with a walk-off home run.

The Angels' Garret Anderson became the first player in history to, in either order, get four hits in a game at Fenway Park and four hits in a game at Yankee Stadium.

Sean Gallagher became the first pitcher in twenty-six years to hit two batters with the bases loaded in the same game. The last pitcher was Randy Jones, who hit Terry Kennedy twice with the bases loaded in 1982.

Josh Hamilton was walked intentionally with the bases loaded by Tampa Bay's Grant Balfour. It was only the second intentional walk with the bases loaded since divisional play began in 1969; Barry Bonds was the other in 1998. And, according to late baseball historian Jerome Holtzman, it was only the fourth time since 1900 that there has been an intentional walk with the bases loaded.

We had a major league first: 6'10" Randy Johnson was replaced on the pitching mound by 6'11" Jon Rauch, the tallest pitchers in history ever to pitch back-to-back in a big-league game.

10. BOX SCORES

Valenzuela Is Pitching on Thursday

A MYSTERIOUS PACKAGE arrived at my house on a cold March day in 2015. It was so big and unwieldy, I struggled to open it, but when I finally did, I was shocked and amazed and thrilled: it was a box score, a 10-pound, 3-by-3-foot box score with white writing on a green metal background. It was the box score of the 30-3 game in which the Rangers beat the Orioles on August 22, 2007, the only game since 1900 in which a team scored 30 runs, a game over which I made a complete fool of myself as I hysterically explained its historic significance on *Baseball Tonight*, with hilarious background laughter provided by John Kruk.

I love box scores. I always have. So much so that for twenty years, from Opening Day 1990 until the final day of the 2009 season, I clipped every box score of every major league game from the nearest newspaper, and taped each box score into a four-subject spiral notebook, a daily task that I have estimated, at approximately fifteen minutes a day, cost me forty days of my truly pathetic life. And so on Opening Day 2010, a completely irrelevant, epically ridiculous, and spectacularly unimportant streak silently ended, as it should have. Over those twenty years, I never missed one day of clipping and taping box scores, a streak that even our best baseball fans must acknowledge is far more impressive than Cal Ripken playing in 2,632 consecutive games. On one memorable night in 2002, I went to bed at eleven o'clock, realized in horror that I had forgotten to do my box score book, got dressed, clipped and taped my box scores, then lay down for six restful hours of sleep as my wife looked at me and wondered how she could have married such an unfathomable geek.

I now know what Joe DiMaggio felt like when his 56-game hitting streak ended on July 17, 1941. He was stopped by Indians third baseman Ken Keltner's two great defensive plays; my equally unbreakable streak—who would want it?—was stopped by the slow demise of the newspaper business, the business I grew up in, the business I will always love. But in 2009, it became clear that my *Washington Post*, due to deadline issues, was no longer providing enough box scores in its home edition. When only seven boxes out of fifteen made it to my driveway at 6 a.m., part of the next twenty-four hours were spent tracking down the missing ones because, I felt, if you are missing one box score, you are missing them all—the set must be complete. So it was great consternation, I decided that 2009 would be my last year.

I probably should have quit my obsession in 2004 when I returned home from a trip to discover what should have been considered an omen, a sign to become less obsessive than Dustin Hoffman in *Rain Man*: "Valenzuela is pitching on Wednesday." My closet was in shambles; the top shelf had collapsed from the weight of fifteen years of box score books, two books per year, a total of thirty. My God, all those 3-for-4 games by Wade Boggs and Tony Gwynn were covered with plaster! My suits that I wore on *Baseball Tonight* were in a heap, caked with drywall, which wouldn't be a big deal except it's hard to find 36-short suits other than at Nordstrom for Kids.

But I was saved, as always, by my brother Matt, who rebuilt my closet, and I continued my preposterous quest to capture every box score. My wife reminded me several times over the later years that box scores were available on the Internet, something I was keenly aware of, but being an old newspaper guy, I enjoyed having the hard copy of the box score at the ready, be it in a car, a cab, or a plane. Having every box score of a season at my side wherever I went gave me a great sense of comfort. If, for example, I wasn't sure how the Padres were using their bullpen I would go through a month of Padres box scores, and then I would know. In 1993, about the time of the start of the Steroid Era, I counted by hand from my box score book the number of players that had gotten four extra base hits in a game that season, a task that would have taken the Elias Sports Bureau eight seconds, but that took me a flight from Dallas to San Francisco. But I couldn't have done it without my box score book, and it was more satisfying than reading the *SkyMall* magazine.

Without my book, I read box scores from the newspaper, and for the missing ones, I read them on ESPN.com. I've saved money on Scotch tape and scissors; after 9/11, I lost six pairs of scissors because I forgot to remove them from my computer bag, and airport security thought I might try to hijack the plane using scissors as dull as an NFL preseason game.

I still read the box scores with the same vigor and intensity every day because there is so much to learn from them; there are so many answers in the box scores and they so enhance my love of the game. Twice a year, I have lunch with Dr. George Will and Dr. Charles Krauthammer, who write and speak about important issues in the world, such as politics and war and gay marriage. But at lunch, all we talk about is baseball, which is good because I can't talk fluently about anything else, especially with two guys that, when it comes to intelligence, make me feel like Fred Flintstone.

At lunch one day, Charles said, without apology, "I read the front page for ninety seconds every day, then I go straight to the box scores."

To which, George said, "Why do you waste the ninety seconds?"

Former major league manager Gene Mauch once showed me how to determine which player made the last out of the game by reading a box score, calculating the at bats, runners left on base, double plays, etc. Mauch had better things to do, yet that intrigued him, so it intrigued me that one of the most brilliant managing minds in baseball would sit at breakfast and determine that Dan Ford made the last out in the Orioles–KC game last night.

I start every day with the box scores because there's always a chance there will be a batting or pitching line that I have never seen before, and might never see again, such as Clayton Kershaw's 9-0-0-0-0-15 in 2014, making him the only pitcher in major league history to throw a no-hitter with no walks and 15 strikeouts. And in that same season, the Braves' Jason Heyward became the only player ever to steal three bases in a game in which his team was no-hit. And in 2011, in then-Angel Ervin Santana's no-hitter, the final line for the Indians—runs, hits, and errors—was 1-0-5, the only such line in baseball history.

If you look closely enough, the box score lines produce all sorts of history, some of it important, some of it so stupid, only a dope like me would be interested. Every day, I check to see if anyone had what I call a reverse triple-double, that is, two errors, two strikeouts, and two grounded into double plays in one game. My best friend in the whole world, Ken Hirdt of the Elias Sports

Bureau, went back to 1933 in the National League (when GIDPs were first kept) and 1940 in the American League (when GIDPs were first kept) and found only one guy with a reverse triple double: Kurt Bevacqua in 1978. That was two years before I started covering Major League Baseball. So I will continue to look daily, and when I find the next guy, I surely will catapult from my seat and scream with joy.

Even though I now have a 10-pound reminder of that famous 30-3 box score hanging in my home, I still keep a smaller copy—a gift from the official scorer that day, Mark Jacobson—in the top left drawer of my home office. I still just like to look at that box score, including the batting line of the eighth and ninth hitters in the Rangers lineup, Jarrod Saltalamacchia's 6-5-4-7 and Ramon Vazquez's 6-4-4-7, which has to be the only game in history in which the eighth and nine hitters each had seven RBIs. And I still get reminded by someone, at least weekly, about my breathless reaction that day on ESPN, and the uncontrollable laughter in the background by Kruk, who couldn't believe that anyone could be brought to such hysteria by the sight of a box score that had never been seen in baseball history.

I will always devour the daily box scores, but I don't miss the black ink on my fingers, lugging around a notebook the size of a phone book, and the look of disbelief from my wife that a grown man would do such a stupid thing for twenty years. Yet when one of my colleagues, Orel Hershiser, found out that my streak was over, he said, "This is big. You have to write about that." When ex-Padres manager Bud Black found out that I had such a streak, he called me at streak's end to tell me, "You should be proud of yourself. That is amazing."

And something unexpected happened that first year of not cutting out the box scores. I got a number of letters from average fans saying that they had done the same thing that I had done for . . . ten, twenty, thirty years. I told a sportswriter friend from Minneapolis, Jim Souhan, that there were days that first year that I would look for my box score book by my side, it wasn't there anymore, and I missed it. Over which, he later told me, "You made me cry."

As it turns out, box scores are so personal and important, they can make you cry. And I nearly cried when that enormous box score arrived at my house courtesy of some fan named Christopher Black, who years ago had e-mailed me with a baseball question, which I had happily answered, followed by his question: what is my favorite box score ever? I replied with the 30-3 game, and two years later, as a present for what he termed my "love for the game," he, through ESPN, sent a package to my house, a box score in a giant box.

With great care, and help, I hung that box score in our basement, which has a baseball theme to it. So as I sit and watch games on our sectional couch, above my right shoulder sits, among other delicacies, the batting lines of the Rangers' Jarrod Saltalamacchia (6-5-4-7) and Ramon Vazquez (6-4-4-7), which is the only game in major league history in which the eighth and ninth hitters in the order each had seven RBIs. When I look at the big green box score, which I often do, I don't cry. I smile. Thank you, Christopher Black, for the reward for twenty years of service that no other adult grown male would have ever even considered.

It was a pleasure. And a daily task than can only happen in baseball.

11. OBITS

Tonight, He Made Me Cry

THE 2014 WORLD Series was briefly halted when the news crossed during Game 5 that Oscar Taveras, 22, a rising out-fielder for the St. Louis Cardinals, had died in a car crash in the Dominican Republic. In baseball, as in life, death stops everything, especially when it involves someone so young. It has a devastating effect on a team and a city, especially a team such as the Cardinals, who are so involved in the lives of their players, and especially in a city such as St. Louis, where Cardinal base-ball is more than important, it is intimate.

When a baseball player dies, a member of the baseball family dies—that's how much time teammates spend together during the course of the season. When Cardinals pitcher Darryl Kile died suddenly in 2002 hours before a Cardinals–Cubs game at Wrigley Field, Cubs player representative Joe Girardi made the announcement with tears in his eyes that that day's game would be postponed. When one of the young sons of Orioles infielder Tim Hulett died after being hit by a car, the Orioles had to play a game that night. "No one wants to play tonight," Oriole outfielder Brady Anderson told me. "It's like one of our children died."

When someone in the game dies, it is important to explain what that person meant to his team and to the game. Over the last few years, four people that meant a lot to the game, and a lot to me because of how they enhanced my love for the game, died. Nothing is harder than writing an obituary for someone you know, but it is right to offer a proper good-bye.

Tony

On the famed night in 1999 at Fenway Park when the Major League All-Stars surrounded Ted Williams in a spontaneous, emotional, unforgettable pregame gathering, the player that led the contingent to the mound was, predictably, Tony Gwynn because, after Williams, no one understood, or loved, the art of hitting more than Tony Gwynn. "Guys were hesitant to approach him," Gwynn said. "I told them that Ted loved to talk baseball."

No one loved talking about the game more than Tony Gwynn, and in my thirty-five years covering the game, I enjoyed talking to him more than anyone. Our first formal interview came nearly thirty years ago, but it was anything but formal. Everything was informal with Gwynn. My subject that day was the rising strikeout rate. Gwynn growled and said, "I hate striking out. I really hate it. I'd rather ground a ball back to the pitcher." And we were off, a conversation had begun, not a question-and-answer period, and Gwynn was funny, insightful, and interested. He was always like that, including the night he called me back when I was out with friends at a restaurant. He called in the middle of dinner, but when Tony Gwynn calls, you take the call no matter where you are, so I did the interview from the quietest place in the restaurant that I could find, a bathroom stall. Later that night, one of my friends asked, "Who was that guy you were talking to in the bathroom?"

"That was Tony Gwynn," I said.

"You interviewed Tony Gwynn *in the bathroom?*"

Yes. He was always easy to talk to, no matter where you were, no matter where he was, as long as the subject mattered to him, and if it was baseball, it mattered. If it was about hitting, the conversation might never end. His talks with Williams were legendary, because Gwynn could return all of Williams's volleys about hitting while so many other players, including some great hitters, couldn't because they were intimidated by Williams. Not Gwynn.

"He used to tell me, 'Careers are made on the inside part of the plate,'" Gwynn said. "He'd say, 'If a pitcher makes a mistake there, make him pay.' Man, I loved talking to him."

That's because Gwynn is the best hitter, for average, since Williams: Gwynn's career average was .338, the 17th highest of all time, but of that group, only he and Williams played after 1939. Gwynn had 3,141 hits. Gwynn won eight batting titles; only Ty Cobb won more. Gwynn batted .300 for 19 straight seasons; only Cobb had a longer streak. From 1993 to '97, Gwynn hit .368—Williams never hit that high for any five-year period. And during that five-year period, Gwynn hit an astonishing .335 when he had two strikes. During those five years, only Mike Piazza hit that high using *all* of his strikes.

Gwynn's hits went everywhere, but he especially liked slashing singles between the third baseman and shortstop. That's why he had 5.5 written on the tongue of his spikes, because it reminded him at every at bat of the 5.5 hole, the hole between the third baseman and shortstop: when in doubt, hit a hard ground ball between there. Put it in play somewhere. In twenty years, Gwynn struck out only 434 times; some players today reach that in just over two seasons. Gwynn never struck out more than 40 times in any season; three players did that in April 2013. In his career, Gwynn had 297 three-hit games, and one three-strikeout game.

Gwynn's bat control was legendary partly because in the last ten years of his career, he used a tiny bat: 33 inches, 30½ ounces, which he needed because his hands were remarkably small. So small, in fact, that he couldn't palm a basketball, yet he started as point guard for four years at San Diego State, and graduated as the school's all-time leader in assists. He needed a little bat because his little hands couldn't control anything bigger, and bat control was what Gwynn was all about. Gwynn referred to his bats as Seven Grains of Pain.

Gwynn was an artist; his bats were his magic brushes. He told me he once visited the Louisville Slugger factory, and selected the billets of wood used for his bats. One of his teammates with the Padres, Scott Livingstone, used the exact same model bat, identical weight and length. And yet, Gwynn would close his eyes and have me hand a bat to him, then tell me whether it was his bat or Livingstone's. I did the test with him with five bats, and he guessed all five correctly. One of those bats he used almost exclusively for the entire 1994 season, a season in which he batted .394, but because of the baseball strike that year, he was denied a shot to become the first player to hit .400 since Williams in 1941. The only time Gwynn didn't use his favorite bat in 1994 was against a left-hander such as Jeff Fassero, who could get in on Gwynn's hands, and possibly break his bat.

"I loved that bat," Gwynn said. "The next spring training,

I broke it taking batting practice on a back field against Peach [Padres coach Rob Picciolo]. I almost started to cry."

"So did I," Picciolo said.

Gwynn was such a great hitter in part because he could see the ball better than anyone else, and therefore was able to wait a hundredth of a second longer than everyone else to start his swing, which is why he never seemed to be off balance at the plate. During batting practice before Game 1 of the 1998 World Series at Yankee Stadium, Gwynn, then 38, stormed out of the cage and yelled to no one in particular, "I can't see at all like I used to!"

"What, is your vision only 20-20 now?" I asked.

"No," he said, "it's 20-15, and I can't see at all like I used to!"

Gwynn told me he could see the split-fingered-fastball grip used by Astros pitcher Shane Reynolds even before Reynolds took the ball out of his glove to throw. I asked if anyone else could see that. "No," Gwynn said. He said he could see Randy Johnson's famous slider pretty well, and said it was easier for a left-handed hitter to hit Johnson's slider than a right-handed hitter. To which, Adam Dunn, a left-handed hitter, laughed and said respectfully, "That's asinine. No left-handed hitter could hit that slider except Tony Gwynn."

Gwynn knew his swing so well. He knew everyone's swing. Outfielder Al Martin joined the Padres midway through his career, soon after he had started hitting the ball to the opposite field with power, but he didn't know why he was now able to do that. So Gwynn took him to the batting cage and showed him why, meaning Gwynn knew more about Al Martin's swing than Al Martin knew about his own swing. Gwynn worked constantly off a batting tee; it was the first thing he did every day, it was his way of getting his hands and his swing ready for every game.

One day he set up a batting tee at the back of home plate, put a ball on it, and explained to teammate Greg Vaughn that Vaughn could let the ball travel that deep in the strike zone and still hit the ball with power to the opposite field.

"I can't," Vaughn said. "It's too deep."

"No, it's not," Gwynn said.

Vaughn finally was convinced, and hit 50 homers the next year.

Gwynn was as smart a hitter as anyone since Williams. He was the first hitter ever to really use video to study his swing and the tendencies of pitchers. Today, hitters can watch all their at bats at any time on their phone, but back in the early to mid-1980s, while he was on the road, Gwynn would have his wife, Alicia, tape the Padres games on those clunky VHS tapes. Then Gwynn would take those tapes back on the road with him in a huge trunk. "He bought all the equipment himself," said Bob Geren, a former teammate. "When we would go on the road, he would set up everything himself in a room in the visiting clubhouse. He didn't have a video guy do it for him. It was funny. The best hitter in baseball would be standing on a folding chair hooking up cords so he could watch his videos."

But Gwynn was so much more than a .338 lifetime hitter. He won five Gold Gloves in right field; few right fielders were better than Gwynn at going to the line, fielding a ball, and throwing accurately to second base to hold the hitter to a single. Gwynn stole 319 bases, including 56 in 1987. He is the only player in the last eighty-three years to hit .338 with 300 stolen bases. He passed that speed and defense along to his son, Anthony Jr., who made it to the major leagues in 2004, which might have been the proudest day of Tony Gwynn's life. But I once asked Tony if

Anthony was a faster runner than Tony when Tony was in his prime.

Respectfully, without pretense, Tony said, "No."

Could he throw better? "No," Tony said.

Was he a better outfielder? "No," Tony said.

Tony Gwynn was a dazzling athlete, and in retirement, he returned to his alma mater, San Diego State, to coach the baseball team. Unlike Ted Williams, who was far more interested in teaching hitting than anything else, Gwynn taught his young players the value of speed, defense, and the all-round game. But he could teach hitting as well as anyone. In his final year as a college coach, he was sick and heavy, but he still had those great hands at the plate. "We were struggling," one of Gwynn's players said. "Tony got frustrated. He got in the cage and showed us what we were doing wrong. He was 50 years old, he was way overweight, and he got in the cage and just hit line drives all over the field."

That was Tony Gwynn. His first hit came in 1982, a double off Sid Monge. When Gwynn reached second base, Phillies first baseman Pete Rose warned him, "Hey, kid, don't pass me in one night." Gwynn didn't become only the all-time hit leader, he became the best hitter since Ted Williams, he became Mr. Padre, he became one of the great ambassadors for the game.

The day he was inducted into the Hall of Fame with Cal Ripken—how appropriate is that?—Cooperstown set an induction day attendance record that might never be broken. That weekend, I spoke with dozens of Padres fans that had come thousands of miles to see their baseball hero, the great number 19. One woman wearing a Gwynn jersey joyfully weeped when Gwynn spotted her, hugged her, wiped away her tears, and said, "Thank you."

No, Tony, for all the years, thank *you*.

Zim

The Rangers were riding a 13-game losing streak when a young beat writer dragged himself into manager Don Zimmer's office on yet another scorching day in Texas in May 1982.

"What's wrong with you?" Zimmer said with that famous Zim glare.

"Covering this team isn't as much fun as I thought it would be," the writer said.

"Ah, quit complaining," Zimmer snapped. "Look at you. You're young, you have your whole life ahead of you. Look at me. I'm old, I'm fat, I'm bald, I'm ugly, I have a plate in my head. And I have *this* team to manage. *I'm* the one with the worries."

And then he flashed that Zim smile, that unmistakable, moon-faced smile that could light up a room, especially one in which baseball was spoken. No one, but no one, loved the game more than Don Zimmer. He married his beloved wife, Soot, at home plate in Elmira, New York. He wore a uniform for sixty-six years as a player, coach, and manager. He won a World Championship with the Dodgers in 1955, he managed the Red Sox during their epic collapse in 1978, he managed the Cubs to an unlikely division title in 1989, and, as Joe Torre's bench coach for many years with the Yankees, he became the game's grandfather, baseball's Buddha. In his final job, as a senior advisor for the Rays, he was revered.

The day he died, Zimmer was perhaps the mostly widely loved and respected person in the game. For Zimmer's last few years, Jim Leyland, a former Tigers manager, called him on the phone every day, sometimes two or three times, just to check in and to pick his brain.

"I love Zim," Leyland said.

Most everyone who knew him, loved him. I will remember

him as the manager who told me that day in 1982 to shut up and write, to just be thankful to have a job in baseball. I will remember him as the ultimate gambler, a guy that loved to go to the track, and that didn't manage by the book: in 1982, I saw him walk the Twins' Kent Hrbek with the bases empty with two outs in the ninth inning with a 1-run lead (it worked), and twice that year, I saw him hit-and-run with the bases loaded (without luck), something I'd never seen before or since.

Mostly, I will remember him as the toughest man—in every way—whom I ever met in a major league uniform. His first nickname was Popeye because his arms were huge, and he was short and squat and strong and feisty. In the famous Yankee–Red Sox fight in the 2003 playoffs, Zimmer, then 72, went after Boston pitcher Pedro Martinez, who threw him to the ground (Pedro later said he regretted doing that). Zimmer said that night, "I embarrassed myself, I shouldn't have done that," but he never backed down from a fight. Never.

He was savaged in Boston in 1978 when the Red Sox blew a 14½-game lead over the Yankees, losing in a one-game playoff, a game in which Bucky Dent hit a famous three-run homer. Red Sox pitcher Bill Lee, who nicknamed Zimmer "The Gerbil," criticized him for the way he ran the pitching staff that year. But Zimmer overcame that, as he did everything, always with a laugh and a strong sense of self. After being fired by the Red Sox, Zimmer became a coach with the Yankees, and rented Bucky Dent's house in New Jersey.

"Over the top of my bed," Zimmer said with a classic laugh, "there was a framed newspaper story with the headline: 'Sox Dented.' I went to bed every night with that hanging over my head."

After Boston, some thought Zimmer would never manage again, but he kept coming back for more, no matter how painful the losses. "I can't help it," he said. "I love it." He next managed the flailing Cubs, and took them from 77 wins in 1988 to 93 wins and the division title in 1989, for which he was named National League Manager of the Year. "I missed a sign one time that year," said Phillies manager Ryne Sandberg. "Zim waited until everyone in the dugout was listening, then he screamed at me for missing a sign." Zimmer showed the whole team that if he could yell at Sandberg, he could yell at anyone

It didn't end well with the Cubs, but again, Zimmer never showed a weakness.

Here's how strong he was.

In a minor league game in Columbus, Ohio, in 1952, Zimmer was hit in the head—no helmets back then—by a Jim Kirk fastball that he never saw. When Zimmer woke from a coma, his wife, Soot, and his parents were standing by his bed. His vision was so blurred, he saw three of each. "I thought it was the next day," Zimmer said. "But I'd been out for thirteen days." When he left the hospital after thirty-one days, he had lost 42 pounds (down to 128) and had four holes drilled in his skull, supported by a plastic plate. Soot had to hold his hand when he walked— on a good day, he could make it 50 yards. He almost didn't make it. Period.

"I was this close [to dying]," he said, holding his index and middle finger a half inch apart.

He played the next year.

"You know what the pitchers did?" Zimmer said. "They threw at me to see if I was scared."

He wasn't.

"I moved closer to the plate," he said.

In 1956, Zimmer was hit in the face again, this time purposely, he said, by Hal Jeffcoat, who never once called to check on him. "My face caved in," Zimmer said. "They put a hundred needles in my face to get rid of the black blood." His retina was detached. He was blindfolded for six weeks. He had to feel for his food; many times, he stabbed his chin with his fork. His children weren't allowed to touch him—the slightest nudge could cause more damage to the eye. After six weeks, he was allowed to wear slate glasses, which had pinholes. "I was the happiest guy in the world," Zimmer said. "I could watch TV."

Zimmer came back and played the next year. He played nineteen years in the major and minor leagues. He says he was "lucky," not courageous. He was modest; he was wrong; he was strong.

That toughness came from growing up playing three sports in high school in Cincinnati. He was a great high school football player. His son, Tom, was a terrific high school football player, also, and remembers his father's voice piercing through the crowd every game: *Hit somebody!* Tom Zimmer was also the team's kicker. "I had a game-winning field goal one night," Tom said. "My father was standing right behind the goalpost, he was the only spectator back there, and he had his arms crossed with the look of, 'You better not miss this!' In the huddle, one of my teammates said, 'Do you see your dad behind the goalpost?' I did. I kicked it right over his bald head, and we won that game."

I saw Zimmer's competitiveness, his loyalty, and his sense of humor in 1982 when I covered his Ranger team, which was indescribably bad. During that 13-game losing streak, Zimmer was ordered by ownership to meet individually with his players to discuss short-term goals, an insulting directive that came from a front-office numbskull who said that marketing a baseball team was the same as marketing a tube of toothpaste. So Zimmer had to call in his players and ask how many hits each thought they'd get in their next 25 at bats.

Outfielder Leon Roberts, who was hitting under .200, told Zimmer, "I think I'll get 17 hits."

"That's a lot of hits," Zimmer said.

When the Rangers finally broke that 13-game losing streak, the phone rang in his office.

Zimmer picked up the phone.

"Yes, Mr. President," he said, laughing.

Later that summer, Zimmer was fired on a Monday morning, but was asked as a favor to Rangers owner Eddie Chiles to manage the team Monday, Tuesday, and Wednesday night because Chiles didn't have a replacement. Out of loyalty, Zimmer agreed. When he was officially fired, he took his coaches, some of the clubhouse guys, and the beat writers out to dinner at a local Arlington restaurant called Mr. Catfish. Late in the night, Brad Corbett, the former owner of the Rangers, took off his watch—a Rolex—and gave it to Zimmer.

"I can't accept this," Zimmer said. "I already have a watch. I've had it for twenty years."

Zimmer was a proud man, a simple man, a man always in search of the next competition, whatever it might be. One day in 1982, he took me to the on-deck circle before a game, got in a wrestler's crouch, put his hands out in front of him, and said, "Okay, we're going to fight now. No one leaves this circle, only one man comes out alive, this is a fight to the death."

"I would rather fight a Martian," I said. "You would kill me in two seconds."

The last time I saw Don Zimmer was in September 2013 in the stands at Tropicana Field. He looked old and tired, dragged down from weekly dialysis. He hadn't played golf in years, he couldn't stay for all nine innings of a game, he needed help getting around the ballpark. For the first time in my life, I saw someone other than the rough, tough Don Zimmer.

"Do you think I could beat you now in a fight in the circle?" I said.

"I'm done," he said. "Even *you* could beat me now."

And then he gave me that famed Zim smile. It will always be my final image of him.

Earl

The last time I spent significant time with Earl Weaver was in March 2012. He was old and slow and needed a guy to walk with him in case he fell, but mentally, he was still the same Earl. We were watching an Orioles intra-squad game from the first row of seats in Sarasota, Florida, when manager Buck Showalter quietly called me over to alert me to a play, a tribute, of sorts, to Earl. Seconds later, the Orioles ran a pickoff play, one that Earl had invented in the late '60s. "Hey," Earl yelled at me, "that's *my* pickoff play!"

It was vintage Earl: always ahead of the game, never missed a trick, brilliant, irascible, indomitable, hilarious; he was Mickey Rooney in a baseball uniform. That day in the stands in Sarasota, it was like it was 1979, the first time that I ever met him. Only this time, I was sitting next to him as he dissected the game. In thirty-five years of covering baseball, no one taught me more about the game than Earl. My most cherished days as a writer were the days before a game, sitting on the Orioles bench, listening to, and watching, Earl.

A case could be made that he is the third greatest manager of all time, behind only Joe McCarthy and the legendary Connie Mack. In seventeen years as a manager, all for Baltimore, Weaver went 1,480-1,060 in his Hall of Fame career. He won four pennants and one World Series. He won 90 games 11 times. He won 100 games three years in a row, averaging 106 victories 1969–71. As the Oriole bus left Kansas City after a rare loss in 1970, Earl crackled from the front seat, "Damn, it's hard to stay 50 games over .500!"

He was just smarter, in a simplistic way, than the rest. He built those Orioles teams around pitching, defense, and three-run homers because that's how you win games. Mental mistakes infuriated him; you had to hit the cutoff man, and it was imperative to always keep the double play in order. He hated to bunt because, as he always said, "You only get 27 outs, don't give any one of them away." It angered him when the other team was trying to bunt, and his pitcher wouldn't throw a strike. He would scream, "They're *giving* us an out, throw the ball over the plate!" In 1986, when Angels manager Gene Mauch bunted in the first inning with his number 3 hitter (Wally Joyner), Weaver looked at me the next day and said, respectfully but purposefully, "I could lose my next 500 games, and I'd still have a better record than that guy."

Weaver implored his pitchers to never intentionally throw at a hitter because, "It might lead to a fight. And if there's a fight, our guys and their guys are going to get ejected, and our guys are better than their guys, so we're going to lose on that exchange. So, don't hit them!" A writer made the mistake of constantly asking when Orioles outfielder Al Bumbry, whom Weaver loved, was coming off the disabled list. Earl yelled at the writer, "As far as I'm concerned, Bumbry is dead! I only deal with the living! When he's ready to come off the DL, then he's ready. Until then, he's dead!" To Earl, the DL was indeed the "Dead List."

Weaver was the master of when to call a team meeting, and what to say. But there were very few team meetings because his teams were always so good and, as he once asked me, "What if we have a team meeting and we lose? What do I do then?" He was also the master of running a bullpen; he always knew when to bring in a reliever, when to remove a starter; he knew how to protect his pitchers. One night in Toronto, the Orioles were getting clobbered. Weaver called the bullpen in the sixth inning. His backup catcher, Elrod Hendricks, who was warming up the Oriole pitchers, answered the bullpen phone.

"You better get ready," Weaver said.

"Earl," Hendricks said, "it's me, Elrod."

"I *know* who it is, you better get up!" Weaver yelled.

So Hendricks was brought in to pitch the sixth and seventh innings so as not to burn a real pitcher.

Weaver would gladly tell us those stories as we sat on the bench before games, or in his office after games, which is why he had a great rapport with the writers. In the 1970s, when the Orioles were playing a getaway game on the road, he sometimes would supply his beat writers with what they called "if quotes" before the game. "If we win tonight," he would say, "I'll say, 'Well, we won six out of nine on this trip, we're still four games ahead in the division, and now we're going home.'" That way, the writers could have their stories written almost as soon as the game ended, giving them time to get on the Orioles charter. One Orioles beat writer in the '60s, long before computers, occasionally would show Weaver a printout of the story he had written that night as the team was flying to the next city. Weaver looked at one story and wrote on it, "D+. Shows improvement."

The writers loved Earl because he was so quotable, so funny. One day in Detroit in 1986, Orioles starter John Habyan, just up from the minor leagues, walked the first four Tigers he faced, then was pulled from the game. I casually asked Earl after the game, "So, Habyan was a little off with his control, huh?" Weaver said, "Yeah, I guess home plate at Triple-A is 17 feet wide, not 17 inches! I guess every hitter at Triple-A is about 8 feet tall!"

Not all the players loved Earl, but they all played hard for him. Terry Crowley was a bench player, a terrific pinch-hitter, for Weaver in the 1970s. Weaver once said of him, "I saved his career. If it wasn't for me, Crowley would be working in a beer hall." That quote made it into the newspapers in Baltimore. Crowley was crushed and, nearly in tears, asked Weaver if he had said that. Weaver looked at the quotes, and instead of saying they were taken out of context, he said, "Yeah, those are my words." Then Weaver took Crowley in his office and smoothed things over because he knew he would need Crowley at his best in a key spot that night.

Orioles outfielder Pat Kelly decided, while he was playing, that he was going to be a minister. So, he felt he should tell his manager about his plans. Kelly waited for the right time, a quiet time, to approach Weaver with the big, important news. "Earl," he said, "I'm going to walk with the Lord."

"I'd rather you walked with the bases loaded!" Weaver said.

When the Orioles acquired power-hitting catcher Earl Williams from the Braves in the early 1970s, Weaver had him start the first four exhibition games that first spring so he could get used to catching the great four starters in the Orioles rotation. Before that fourth game, Williams barged into Weaver's office and said, "Don't we have any more fucking catchers on this team?" Weaver later said, "I knew right then that we were in big trouble." Williams played two years with the Orioles, then he was gone, done as a good player.

The players didn't always like the way that Weaver dealt with them, but they couldn't argue with his success, or with his logic. The concept of platoon baseball was originally founded in the early 1900s, but Weaver was the first to popularize it in his seventeen years as a manager. He had batter-pitcher matchups on white index cards always next to him in the dugout, so he would always have the right guy for the right spot. In the eighth inning of Game 1 of the 1979 League Championship Series, the Angels brought in reliever John Montague. He had been acquired late in the season, so Weaver didn't have a white card on him. So Weaver breathlessly called the press box looking for 20-year-old intern Charles Steinberg, who was responsible for, among other things, the data for the white cards.

"I don't have Montague!" Earl yelled.

A panicked Steinberg worked quickly to look up Montague's numbers, then gave the white card to Earl's daughter, Kim, who was an Oriole BaseBell, a person who, among other duties, helped deliver things, such as soft drinks, during games. She had never delivered a key piece of information to her father during a game. So she rushed down from the press box, through the Oriole clubhouse (where she'd never been allowed), past Jim Palmer, who was wearing only a towel, and into the dugout. Weaver saw it: the guy to use against Montague was John Lowenstein, who was 3 for 4 against him with two homers. Lowenstein pinch-hit against Montague, and hit a three-run homer to win the game.

The umpires hated Earl, and for the most part, he hated them. On Earl Weaver Day at Memorial Stadium after Weaver retired (for the first time) after the 1982 season, he rode on the back of a convertible around the stadium, waving to the crowd. One umpire said that day, "If there is a God, that little SOB will fall off the back of that convertible and get run over." Weaver was ejected just short of 100 times in his career, and virtually every one of them was volcanic and entertaining. He told me that he would turn his cap around backward to argue "so I wouldn't accidentally hit the umpire with the bill of my cap. No contact. With contact, I could get suspended." The crowds at Memorial Stadium went wild when Earl went wild because the fans and players knew he was standing up for them.

Weaver retired again, and for good, after the 1986 season. He didn't have a good team that year, and losing really bothered him. Early on a Sunday morning in September in Oakland that year, he filled out his lineup card in the midst of a horrible collapse the final two months of that season. "Tim," he said, "this is the worst lineup card I've ever filled out in a major league game." Three weeks later, he would manage his last game, in a Hall of Fame career that finished under an avalanche of losses. But that in no way took away from his legacy as one of the greatest managers of all time. In the summer of 2012, the Orioles dedicated a statue to all their Hall of Famers, and Weaver's statue stands among those of Brooks Robinson, Frank Robinson, Jim Palmer, Cal Ripken, and Eddie Murray, all of whom he managed. They will all tell you: no one knew the game better than Earl Weaver.

Earl Weaver died at age 82 on an Orioles cruise, which is fitting because twenty-five years after he retired, he was the highlight of the cruise, the guy that all the old Oriole fans—and the new—wanted to meet. I had the pleasure of knowing him well. And that last day I spent significant time with him, that intrasquad game in Sarasota, was one of the highlights of my writing career. That day, an Orioles outfielder overthrew the cutoff man, allowing the batter/runner to advance to second base with one out. So, instead of runners being at the corners, there were runners at second and third. Weaver was very upset at the outfielder's mistake.

"Damn it," he growled. "The double play isn't in order! You have to keep the double play in order!"

To the end, he was the Earl of Baltimore, the smartest baseball man I've ever met, the great Earl Weaver.

Flanny

I have been frequently asked to name my favorite player, and the funniest player that I have ever covered, and the answer to both questions has been the same since I first met Mike Flanagan in 1979. He was the wittiest, sharpest, most clever baseball player I've ever known, a guy that, no matter the subject, provided perspective and context and a laugh.

"Flanny," as everyone called him, had not been his usual personable, hilarious self in the years after retirement; the many losses he took as the Orioles general manager wore on him, he took them home, and being replaced as GM in 2008 depressed him even more.

He returned to broadcasting in 2010, and soon became one of the best color commentators in the game, but he still wasn't the guy I went to after so many games for a line, a laugh, or an observation. Something was wrong, but no one knew what. And then, on a warm August night in Baltimore in 2011, he took his own life, gone before he turned 60.

I will remember him only with fondness. I will remember him as a great teammate, and a very good pitcher. He won 167 games, and he won the American League Cy Young Award in 1979. He threw a sinking fastball, a terrific curveball; he had a great pick-off move and good control. Asked where that control came from, Flanagan said that, as a teenager, his 72-year-old grandfather would catch him in the backyard of their home in Manchester, New Hampshire. "If I threw too far inside or too far outside, he couldn't reach it," he said. "And if he missed it, he would have to chase it. So I had to learn how to hit the target."

Flanagan always had a story. The Orioles made it to the World Series in 1979. "I got on base in that series," he said. "Jimmy Frey [the Orioles' first-base coach] told me when I got to first, 'Okay, keep your left foot on the bag, and get as big a lead as you can with your right foot.'" The Orioles were a little late running out on the field for one of those World Series games. "People think we were having some team meeting before the game," Flanagan said. "But we were all in the clubhouse waiting for [TV judge] Wapner to deliver his verdict."

In 1980, as another Oriole pitcher, Steve Stone, was on his way to winning the Cy Young, Flanagan determined the different stages of Cy: he was the reigning Cy Young. "[Jim] Palmer is Cy Old," he said. "Stone is Cy Present and Storm [Davis] is Cy Future. When you get hurt, you become Cy-bex. When you're done, you become Cy-onara." Flanagan was great with names. He called Jose Canseco, back when he could mash, "Jose Don't Make a Mistake-o." He called Ruben Sierra, back when he could mash, "Ruben Scare-ya." He called former teammate Don Stanhouse, who was bizarre, "Stan the Man Unusual."

On Opening Day 1986, the Orioles mascot, the Bird, fell off the top of the dugout during the game and had to be helped off the field. As Flanagan left the clubhouse after the game, he said, "I told him to take two worms and call me in the morning." That year, teammate Mike Boddicker threw a good game one night in Toronto; his fastball was clocked at 87 mph. "That's 82 Canadian," Flanagan said, and kept on walking. Flanagan was traded to the Blue Jays in 1987. The following spring, I asked him for the biggest difference between training in Dunedin as compared to the Orioles' spring training facility in a dangerous section of downtown Miami. "No armed guards in the parking lot," Flanagan said.

In his career, Flanagan met several United States presidents, Canadian Prime Minister Brian Mulroney, and the Queen of England. "She left the game in the third inning, everyone else left in the fifth," Flanagan said of a terrible game that featured seven walks and three errors. "Maybe she was more accustomed to baseball than we know." On Opening Day 1991, when he returned to pitch at Memorial Stadium, Flanagan received three standing ovations. "I got a bigger hand than the secretary of defense," he said, referring to Dick Cheney, who attended the game. "And he had a better spring than I did."

I covered a game in 1991 in which Orioles DH/first baseman Sam Horn struck out six times consecutively, the first non-pitcher in AL history to do that. After the game, I went to Flanagan for perspective. "Three strikeouts is a hat trick," he said, "four is a sombrero, five is a golden sombrero, and from now on, six will be known as a Horn. Seven will be a Horn-A-Plenty."

When Memorial Stadium closed down in 1991, after the final game, all the players went to the positions at which they had played for the Orioles. There were two dozen pitchers on the mound when former Orioles catcher Rick Dempsey got behind the plate and put down a sign. Dempsey was terrific defensively, and one of the game's best throwers, but he wasn't a particularly good caller of a game. "All twenty-five pitchers shook him off," said Flanagan.

I will remember Flanagan playing basketball. Few people could shoot a basketball better than him. In July 1987, I casually asked him what he had done during the All-Star break. After much prodding from me, he told me he shot some free throws with his nephew, and made 105 in a row. So, I wrote that in *The Baltimore Sun* the next day. The team was on the road, and Flanagan approached me. "My wife told me that you put that in the paper today," Flanagan said. "I wanted to clarify something: I didn't miss the 106th free throw, my nephew got tired of feeding me, so he quit." Flanagan played basketball in his high school alumni game one year, and scored 63 points. He played freshman basketball at UMass with Rick Pitino. Flanagan tried out for the varsity the next year. "I pulled up for a jumper on the break from the top of the key, and Julius Erving blocked it, then swoop-jammed on the other end," he said. "I knew then it was time to work on my slider."

My favorite Flanagan story came in Toronto in 1987. He was driving to Exhibition Stadium with former teammate Mike Boddicker in a Blue Jays rental car, with the Blue Jays insignia splattered all over it. New players to the team drove these rentals until their cars arrived. Flanagan spotted me as I was walking to the ballpark, lugging my computer and oversized bag of books. He gave me a ride.

"This was Phil Niekro's car," Flanagan said of the ancient pitcher that had just been released.

"How do you know it was his car?" I asked.

"I found his *teeth* in the glove compartment," he said.

No one made me laugh like Mike Flanagan. On a horrible night in August 2011, he made me cry.

12. ESPN

I Shot a Deer in a Hot Tub

It was a random Tuesday night at ESPN in 2010. I was sitting in what we call the War Room watching fifteen games on TV while sitting next to one of our *Baseball Tonight* analysts, Buck Showalter. It was just the two of us, which is how I liked it most. The stuff I learned in that room on those nights I will remember for the rest of my life. Showalter looked at me and asked, "Have you ever seen a great player who has a lot of freckles?"

I had no idea how to respond to such a wonderfully ridiculous question.

"Bobby Kielty," I said without thinking, retracted it, and said, "Rusty Staub."

"I said a 'great player,' not a 'good player,'" Showalter said.

Later in the same night, as we watched Vicente Padilla pitch, I made the mistake of asking Showalter a question before thinking. "Did you ever manage Padilla?" Showalter smiled and said, "We signed him when I was with the Diamondbacks. We went to his hometown in Nicaragua—he came to the signing on a burro. He agreed to our offer, but said he needed another $2,000 because he had to give his burro away when he signed, and he needed

$2,000 to make sure the burro had a good home. So we gave it to him."

Freckles and burros and Buck Showalter: that's why I love working at ESPN. Hot tubs, Robert De Niro, and John Kruk: that's why I love working at ESPN. Impersonations, baseball cards, and Aaron Boone: that's why I love working at ESPN. Hot dog missiles, S'mores, and Terry Francona: that's why I love working at ESPN. I have worked with forty-one former-player analysts over the last twenty years, and the stuff I've learned from the guys that played and managed the game at the highest level is the best part of working on *Baseball Tonight*. Sitting next to Bobby Valentine during a World Series game, or watching 15 games with Buck Showalter in the War Room, is something that all baseball fans should experience. It has made me love and appreciate the game even more because it reminds me again how much I don't know, and how much more they can see in a game than I can. "When you watch a game," Showalter said, "watch what happens away from the ball. What does the right fielder do on a ball to the shortstop, is he moving or just standing there?"

There are experts on almost everything—including worthless things—on *Baseball Tonight*. One night, a nondescript Thursday night in August, ESPN producer Judd Burch, our umpire savant, stopped by the War Room. "Who's working third base tonight in Texas?" I asked Burch. No one would know this. It took him two seconds. "Adrian Johnson," he said. He was right. There is researcher/writer Mark Simon: he knows who made the final out of every World Series back to 1953. There is research executive Jeff Bennett: he can describe, in detail, virtually every Topps baseball card from the years 1980–85.

And then there is John Kruk, who is an expert at being Kruk. He is who you see on TV: a short, squat, strong, fearless, hilarious former baseball player, a proud redneck from West Virginia. "I used to be 5'11"," he told me. "When I was with the Padres, I got in a car crash, I went through the windshield. Now I'm 5'10". Compression, I guess." What you may not know about Kruk is that he is a great singer, he is a great athlete, he is close to a scratch golfer, he was a terrific high school basketball player and, of course, he was a lifetime .300 hitter in ten years in the big leagues. He retired one night in Baltimore in 1995. He got a hit in his final at bat, told the manager that he was done, left the ballpark during the game, and never came back. "Ten days later," Kruk said, "my agent called me and said, 'Are you hurt? I haven't seen you in the lineup for a week.' I said, "No, I retired.' He was pissed."

Kruk often appears pissed, but he's not. He's a big-hearted guy: one day in Maryvale, Arizona, on the ESPN Bus Tour, he brought on a widowed mother and her two children, age 10 and 8, for a tour of the bus, treating them like gold, after which the mom cried and said, "This is the best day of my kids' lives." More often than pissed, he is funny. His stories from growing up in West Virginia, from winter ball, from minor league baseball, and from the big leagues are priceless.

"Did I ever tell you about the time I shot a deer in a hot tub?" Kruk asked me one day on the bus. Because it was Kruk, because you never knew with Kruk, I had to ask, "Were you in the hot tub, was the deer in the hot tub, or were *both* of you in a hot tub?" Kruk said, "I was in high school; I had my shotgun next to the hot tub." He then looked at me for some sort of affirmation, as if he expected me to say, "Yeah, John, that's where I keep *my* shotgun." He said, "I stood up, buck naked, grabbed my shotgun, and shot the deer. Then I sat back down."

That's how most of Kruk's best stories begin. "Did I ever tell you about . . ."

"Did I ever tell you about the movie I did with Robert De

Niro?" he once asked me. Kruk had a very small part in the movie *The Fan*. It was shot in 1995, and he was on location for three months. "De Niro killed me near the end, he stabbed me in the eye with a knife," Kruk said. "He was a great guy, such a nice guy off camera, but when that scene began, he became another person. It was pretty wild. I could see the *Cape Fear* in his eyes."

Another trip, another story . . .

"Did I ever tell you about the commercial I did with Mike Tyson [in 2001]?" Kruk said. "My wife [in the commercial] and I just had a baby, and we're going out one night, and I tell my wife, 'Honey, we have a babysitter.' And in comes Mike Tyson, holding our baby. It was funnier than hell." It was a real baby, and Kruk said that Tyson would not put the child down, saying, "I hate adults, but I love kids. I could spend all day in a nursery."

Another trip, another story . . .

"Did I ever tell you about the time that my roommate in the minor leagues was a bank robber?" Kruk said. "This was about 1987–88. I heard that he robbed anywhere from sixteen to twenty-five banks. I had no idea that he robbed banks. One day, the FBI showed up at our clubhouse before batting practice to question me about it. They'd been tracking him for about a year. They wanted to know if I was an accomplice; I told them that I hadn't robbed any banks. They found him. He called me a couple of times when he was in prison."

One of Kruk's teammates in the minor leagues was the young shortstop Ozzie Guillen. Ozzie said he learned to speak English from Kruk. "He taught me to swear," Ozzie said. As minor league teammates, they once went to a casino in Reno. Kruk was playing blackjack. Ozzie was looking at the hands of other players at the table, then feeding the information to Kruk in Spanish. "Then," Guillen said, "I felt two hands around my throat, I was being choked and dragged out of the casino by the bosses. I screamed at Krukkie: 'Help, please, John.' He turned, looked at me, turned back to the table, and said, 'Hit me.'"

Kruk has a lot of stories about golf.

"Did I ever tell you about the time I nearly killed a lady on the golf course in Vegas?" Kruk said. "I hadn't hit a fairway all day, but on this short par 4—340 yards—I really caught one. My drive hit a lady on the green as she was putting. It fractured her skull. She went right down. She was out. Ambulance. Everything. I felt terrible. She was in the hospital for one night. I called her a few times. She wasn't mad. She said, 'I'd be upset if you hit me in the fairway, but it's not your fault that you hit me off the tee on a 340-yard hole.'"

And, of course, Kruk has a million stories about his days on the crazy 1993 Phillies.

"We were playing one night at Shea [Stadium]," Kruk said. "[Reliever Bruce] Ruffin was throwing in the bullpen. There were cops on horses all over the place. Ruffin hit a horse right in the butt with a pitch. The horse went crazy, as did the other horses around it. It really shook Ruffin up. Mike Ryan, our bullpen coach, called the dugout and told [manager Jim] Fregosi, 'You better get someone else up. Ruffin just hit a horse in the ass.'"

I love working with Kruk, but I also love working with ESPN analyst Aaron Boone. He is as human, as normal, as everyman as any former major leaguer I've ever met, which is impressive given that he hit one of the biggest home runs in the last twenty-five years, and that he is a member of the only three-generation family of All-Stars in major league history. Boone plays fantasy football and baseball, he's quick with a laugh, you can poke fun at him, and he still has his nerdy friends from his middle school years. I met three of those friends at Boone's 40th birthday party in 2013. They had all met him when he moved to Southern

California as a seventh-grader in the early '80s when Bob Boone signed with the Angels. After a month of going to school with him, those three decided that the new kid, the great athlete, "is Bob Boone's son." Indeed. Aaron Boone had never let anyone know that he was the son of the catcher for the hometown Angels.

That's how he is, but he is more than that. He can impersonate and mimic famous people, as well as the producers on *Baseball Tonight*. He does *Saturday Night Live*'s Chris Farley's hysterically funny Matt Foley, Motivational Speaker skit. "In college [at USC]," Boone said, "someone on our team would just come to me and say, 'We need Matt Foley here.' So I would do the 'Livin' in the Van Down by the River' skit for them."

Boone can imitate hundreds of batting stances and pitching motions of players from the late '70s until today. On the *Baseball Tonight* show that I host, I had him do Pete Rose, Larry Bowa, Dave Winfield, Bake McBride, and Tommy John, and every one of them was perfect. The night before the show, he told me he was working on his Joe Torre, which I thought would be Torre as a hitter. But when he did Torre, the manager, shuffling to the mound to take out a pitcher, I fell down laughing on national TV. At our final *Monday Night Baseball* game one season, at the postgame gathering, Boone, in exiting for the night, did his Torre impersonation for those who hadn't seen it, and left the room in hysterics.

I didn't think anyone knew (or cared to know) uniform numbers better than I do, but Boone is as good. Ask him any player's number from about a thirty-year period, and he has a chance.

"Johnny Ray," I said, testing him with a second baseman from the '80s.

"Angels or Pirates," he said without hesitation.

"Pirates," I said.

"Three," he said.

He was correct. He also can look at virtually any baseball card and tell you the ballpark in which the picture was taken. Some of the backgrounds are so fuzzy, they are like looking at a sonogram. Yet Boone, who spent so much time in those ballparks as a kid with his dad, and later as a major leaguer, can find a spot or a color that gives him the answer.

"In what park was this taken?" I asked, showing him a baseball card.

"The new Comiskey," he said. "See the glare on the seats?"

"How do you know that?" I asked.

"There are some things that I just know," he said.

I love working with Kruk and Boonie, but my favorite at ESPN was Showalter, because he is the most prepared, most observant, most passionate baseball man I've ever met. My favorite segment with him on *Baseball Tonight* was one night when he explained what he would look for in a young player, starting with the feet and, moving one body part at a time, finishing at the top of the head.

"Never draft a guy whose feet point like this; that's what we call a 10-to-2 guy," Showalter said, pointing his feet at an angle outward, like 10 minutes until 2 on a clock. "We want the guy whose feet point in, a little pigeon-toed. That's the athlete, that's the runner."

He moved up the human body. "We are looking for a guy with a nice, high butt," Showalter said. "Those guys are the athletes. Dave Winfield had a high butt. You don't want a low butt—a low-butt guy usually can't run. And you want to find a pitcher with a nice V for a back, with broad, straight shoulders. Derek Holland has a V. Look for the V."

Then Showalter got to the head area.

"Never draft a guy with bright blue eyes," he said. "You can't see as well in day games with bright blue eyes." Several years later when Josh Hamilton, then of the Rangers, was struggling terribly trying to hit during day games, he explained that his eyes were so blue, he had trouble seeing during day games. When I was asked the next day on *SportsCenter* if I'd ever heard that, I said, "Yes, Buck told us that three years ago!"

Showalter finished his body scouting report by saying, "Never, ever draft an 18-year-old that has a full beard. That means he's fully grown at 18, he's likely not going to grow anymore. When we drafted Derek Jeter at 18, he didn't even have to shave. I thought, 'We have something here. This guy is going to mature, and get bigger and stronger.' And he did."

These are the things I learned on a nightly basis from Showalter. One night, a left-handed pitcher was holding runners on first and third, but the pitcher never paid attention to the runner on third in part because, when going from the stretch, he couldn't even see the runner. "Alan Embree [a left-handed reliever] was like that," Showalter said. "We [the Diamondbacks] were playing the Giants one night, and before the game, I told Luis Gonzalez, 'Tonight, you are going to get on third base late in the game, and with Embree pitching, you're going to steal home because the way he sets up on the mound, he won't be able to see you leading off third.' Gonzo looked at me like I was crazy. But that night, it all worked out. Embree was in the game late, Gonzo was on third, Embree never saw him, and Gonzo stole home. He came back in the dugout and looked like, 'I can't believe that.'"

One night, we watched a player get out of a rundown. "Deion Sanders played for me," Showalter said. "We ran a rundown drill in spring training. We put him in the middle. He was so fast, so quick, we couldn't tag him out. It defeated the purpose of the drill. So we had to put another runner in the middle, one that wasn't too fast or too quick to tag out."

I can't tell you how many times, as we sat in the War Room at

ESPN, Showalter would look at me and say, "Did you see that?" And, of course, I hadn't seen it. No one sees what Showalter sees. One night, there was a shot from the dugout that showed Cardinals manager Tony La Russa twirling his index finger for a split second to catcher Yadier Molina.

"Watch," Showalter said, "here comes the inside move."

And, on command, Cardinals pitcher Adam Wainwright made the inside move to second base.

Showalter has an acute need for cognition, and not just about baseball. In his final off-season at ESPN, he called me one night because he knew I had played in a rec league basketball game the night before. He called with a list of five questions, all of them rapid-fire.

"What did you eat before the game?"

"What did you play on your car radio on the way to the game?"

"How long before game time did you arrive at the gym?"

"How many assists did you have?"

"Did you drink beer with your teammates after the game?"

I answered all five, rapid-fire. He said, "Thanks, just wanted to know." And then he hung up.

Showalter's inquisitive nature has served him well as the highly successful manager of the Orioles. After taking over in August 2011, his first act was to address the team, a speech he called a B+ speech: "You have to keep your A speech for spring training with the entire team gathered." In that B+ speech, the Japanese interpreter began interpreting—out loud—during the speech, to which Showalter said, "Shut the hell up, I'm talking here!" From that point, he had that team. They all recognized immediately that he was indeed in charge, which was made abundantly clear when one of the first moves he made in his manager's office was to replace a picture above his desk because the picture was of the Orioles in the field, and the opponent had the bases loaded.

"This is a negative picture," he said. "I don't want bases loaded sitting above my shoulder every day." So he had it replaced with another picture, one with a picture of every manager in Orioles history.

The first two months on the job, one of his young players, Josh, Bell, forgot how many outs there were three times. Three times in two months! So Showalter went to him and said, "Josh, you have forgotten how many outs there are three times in the last two months."

"Well," Bell said, "it was only twice."

"How about the time in Kansas City?" Showalter said.

"Oh, you saw that?" Bell said.

"Yeah," Showalter said, "I saw that."

He sees everything, and his players know that. Just like he would look at me in the War Room at ESPN and say, "Did you see that?" he does the same with his players during games. "Oh, he does it all the time," said Orioles first baseman Chris Davis. "He will walk down the bench and ask us all sorts of questions, like if we saw what the third baseman had done with his positioning in the third inning, or what the pitcher was doing with his hands with runners on base. Finally, I had to say to him, 'Buck, I don't see any of this. No one sees any of this. You are the only one who can see any of this.'"

Bobby Valentine can see those things. He spent several years at ESPN and, as with Showalter, I learned so much sitting next to him, watching games, talking about the game. His managing career likely is over—it ended badly after only one year (2012) with the Red Sox—but few know the game better than Valentine, who is an interesting guy. He was a great ballroom dancer in high school, he had his shirts dry cleaned when he was 16, and he was the king of the high school science fair. So, when he explains the maximum break on a curveball, and explains the physics of bat speed, it's because he knows that stuff.

Valentine is fascinated by the game—what players think, what makes them better. What's the best way to make a tag? How do you shield the ball from the sun? He is as perceptive as anyone you will ever meet, constantly looking for ways to get the most from players. "Ichiro is a mathematical genius," he told me. "Because of that, he can read the angles of the field better than everyone else. When he runs to a spot in right field to make a catch, and the ball is there, waiting for him, it's because he can see the angles better than anyone. Plus, I was in an elevator with him once. It was about a forty-floor hotel. He looked at the right side of the elevator, the even numbers, and added them up in his head in, like, two seconds."

Valentine has no patience for some of the clichéd teaching techniques today, and the common misconceptions about the game. Tell him about the "squish the bug" technique that youth hitting coaches teach, and he will squash that theory. He also says that no hitter "swings down on the ball," and says there is no black on home plate, so the pitch can't be "on the black." He says that pitchers don't get "on top of the ball," that's impossible—their hand is on the side of the ball. And don't start him on the "checked swing rule," or the "check swing rule," because, he says, "There is no rule in the rule book for a checked swing. People don't even know what it is. They don't even know how to pronounce it. So how can you call it?"

Valentine has experienced almost everything in the game. He played in the big leagues for ten years, for five teams. He was the number 1 pick of the Dodgers in 1968, taken ahead of Bill Buckner, Davey Lopes, Ron Cey, and Steve Garvey. Valentine won a batting championship in the minor leagues. He also got hit by a pitch in the head, caving in one side of his face. In 1973 for the Angels, he broke his leg after his spike got caught in the outfield wall as he tried to make a catch. The leg improperly healed inside the cast, and the hideous lump on his shin from it is the size of a baseball, an injury that perhaps prevented him from being a very good player (he can't run anymore, which kills him given how fast he used to run after a baseball and with a football). He got to the big leagues briefly at age 19 in 1969, returned two years later. Valentine can laugh now about Dodger manager Walter Alston introducing him as Billy Valentine at the team's Welcome Home Luncheon. A year later, Valentine said, "I introduced Walt to my parents, we were in an elevator. He called me Billy again, right there in front of my parents."

Valentine's best friend and former roommate is Buckner. "[Pitcher] Lloyd Allen got drafted ahead of Buck [by the Angels]," Valentine said. "Buck didn't like him. We were facing Allen in the minor leagues. Buck told me in the on-deck circle, 'I'm going to hit him in the head with a line drive.' First pitch, he hit him right in the head with a line drive."

No one has more stories than Indians manager Terry Francona, who spent one year (2012) as an analyst at ESPN, and we all laughed our entire way through it. His first duty that season was to accompany me on the ESPN Bus Tour in spring training. His first stop that spring was Braves camp, so ESPN had us stay that first night in Orlando at a Disney property called Camp Wilderness. We thought it was a hotel, but as we drove through the wilderness to get there, ESPN indeed had made us stay in individual log cabins at a campsite.

"When I got in the room, there were bunk beds, it was like I was in the Cub Scouts," said Francona, who had won two World Series as the manager of the Red Sox, and was used to staying in better, and different, hotels. "I really believed it was all a big joke.

I really thought, all of a sudden, everyone was going to jump out from behind the curtains and surprise me."

But they didn't.

"Then I called room service," Francona said. "The lady just laughed at me and said, 'Sir, room service at Camp Wilderness is the Coke machine that you saw when you checked in.'"

After a few minutes, Francona called me in my cabin next door.

"Do you want to go out in the backyard to make some S'mores?" he said.

The funniest spring of my life continued the next day at Yankee camp with Francona as a working member of the media. "It's kind of weird being here . . . dressed in a Today's Man, $89 suit . . . pin-striped," Francona said with a laugh. "It's the first time that I have ever said 'Good luck this year' to [Yankee manager] Joe Girardi, and meant it."

As we toured Florida, I asked Francona about being Michael Jordan's manager for the Double-A Birmingham Barons in 1994. "We had the Jordan Cruiser Bus, we traveled in style," Francona said. "We're on a ten-hour trip, and our bus driver had a urinary infection, so he had to go to the bathroom every twenty minutes. So I drove the bus. He said, 'Just keep it straight.' I must have driven that bus a hundred miles. I stayed in one lane. Guys woke up in the middle of the night, and they were like, 'Who the hell is that driving the bus?'"

Two of Francona's players were bragging one day about their basketball skills, "and both guys stink," Francona said. "But MJ's ears perk up. He says 'basketball?' We had a concrete court outside our apartment complex, so we go play to see how good these guys really are. I'm 32 years old, I'm making $29,000 a year, and I'm trying not to get fired. Well, within ten minutes, the radar goes up, everyone knows MJ is in the house, and here come the locals to challenge him. It was MJ and his coaches: really, did it matter? First time down the floor, he made a no-look pass to me, I dislocated a finger, but I was so embarrassed, I didn't tell anyone, I just pulled it back in place. Then an older guy, a bigger guy who had played before, started getting aggressive. MJ cupped the ball at the top of the key, I went to set a screen, he looked at me like 'Get out of my way, you dumb-ass.' I thought, 'This is bad.' He went to the basket, took one dribble, and the next thing you know, the rim was bent, the ball was going through the hoop, and MJ was standing over this guy with that look in his eyes like, 'Not in my house!' Then I said, 'Okay, game's over!'"

Francona laughed.

"MJ is so competitive," he said. "We played Yahtzee on the bus every trip. I know he cheated. He has so much money, but he *had* to win. I'm making $29,000, and he's cheating at Yahtzee!"

I asked Francona how bad the Phillies were when he managed them 1997–2000.

"We were so bad, and we were so young, I wasn't just trying to teach these guys how to play and how to win, but how to be professionals," he said. "My closer was Wayne Gomes. He was a great kid, but he was young, and had so much to learn about the big leagues. So I bring him in from the bullpen and he gets to the mound and he's got mustard all over his jersey. I screamed, 'Gomesy, what are you doing? You can't come into a game with mustard on your jersey!' He said, 'Tito, it wasn't me, some people in the stands threw hot dogs at me when I was leaving the bullpen' . . . and we were at home!"

On our final day in Florida, I asked Francona how his career had ended. The final game of his professional playing career took place for the Cardinals in 1991 on Field 1 at the Blue Jays' spring training facility in Dunedin. Francona was 31 then, he was done physically from so many knee surgeries, and so many other health issues, but was told if he wanted to make the club, he had to play that day and show the brass that he could still at least hit. "That day, I drove in eight runs in an exhibition game," he said. "My final at bat, I fouled a ball off my kneecap. I could barely move. I stayed in the game, and hit a grand slam. Part of my kneecap is still in that batter's box. I could barely run around the bases. I drove in eight runs, and the next day, I was released by the Cardinals. That's how my career ended."

His career as a broadcaster on the ESPN *Sunday Night Game* began with great drama. Minutes before the TV open for the game, Francona, a great athlete, but a klutz beyond comprehension, accidentally got his zipper snagged after going to the bathroom, leaving his fly wide open minutes before going on national TV. He looked at Suzy, the makeup lady, and said, "What should I do?" Suzy got down on her knees in a very compromising and embarrassing position, and with her face buried in Francona's crotch, she repaired his zipper.

"I will never do this again," she said.

And everyone laughed. Francona makes everyone laugh. When someone once asked him to describe the greatness of Fenway Park, he explained that the ballpark is about baseball only, baseball is the only language spoken there. "We don't," he said, "have a bottle of ketchup racing a bottle of mustard and a bottle of relish . . . hey, nothing against ketchup."

That is one of Francona's many gifts, that is what makes him such a great manager, the ability to diffuse difficult and uncomfortable situations and make everyone comfortable by making them laugh. Many years ago at a postgame press conference in the cramped interview room at Fenway Park, a Japanese reporter gallantly tried to ask a question in English but, naturally, struggled

terribly with it. It took a good two minutes of broken English for
him to finish the question, which made everyone uneasy, including
the Japanese reporter. When he was finally done asking the
question, Francona looked at him and said, "You're from Western Pennsylvania, aren't you?" And everyone in the room howled
because the ice was broken, and because Francona is, of course,
from Western Pennsylvania.

Francona is as mischievous as they come, the ultimate practi-
cal joker. He and Red Sox second baseman Dustin Pedroia are
best friends. They played cribbage every day before games, something that players and managers don't do, but Francona was
hardly your normal manager. (Francona later included closer
Jonathan Papelbon in the cribbage games because Papelbon was
a terrible player, and they played for money. "Pap helped me build
a new basement in my house," Francona said.) Francona said he
thought Pedroia, with his balding head, looked like ESPN football reporter John Clayton, a wonderful man, a Hall of Fame
writer, but hardly a good-looking or athletic guy. So Francona
had Clayton, pretending to be Pedroia, tape a rah-rah baseball
speech, which Francona played for his team in the clubhouse.
Everyone, including Pedroia, laughed out loud.

Francona, the prankster, ambushed me on the ESPN Bus Tour
in spring training in 2012. We were in the Blue Jays' tiny clubhouse when pitcher Ricky Romero approached me and said, "You
have to go see [catcher J. P.] Arencibia. He does an impersonation of you." So I went to Arencibia and asked about this im-
pression. Within a minute, the entire Blue Jays team, a good
sixty of them, as well as Francona, were huddled around Arencibia and me as he did his impersonation of my ridiculous voice. I
was so embarrassed, standing in the middle of all of these players, as they laughed uncontrollably at Arencibia's impersonation.
"On the bus going to a spring training games, someone will ask

me to do it," Arencibia told me. "Everyone loves it. I don't impersonate anyone else. Just you, Tim."

Well, that was all Francona needed to hear. He went straight to our TV producer that day, Shawn Fitzgerald, and essentially said, "Fitzy, we need to crush Kurkjian on TV today." So, while I was writing a story on the ESPN Bus, they secretly arranged for Francona and Arencibia to be on camera. In the taped segment, Francona said, "We can't find Kurkjian, but we have his replacement," then proceeded to interview Arencibia doing my voice. So when we did the live *Baseball Tonight* later that day, the last segment was the taped segment of Francona interviewing Arencibia as if he were me. The hysterically funny interview ended with Francona, bent over in laughter, saying, "I can't do this anymore!" Then they came to me on live TV for my reaction to this interview. I didn't know what to say, I was so humiliated, but it was impossible not to laugh. I asked Francona how he could ambush me like that, I lamented that my TV career was over, and I asked, "Is that what I sound like?"

The Arencibia impersonation spread quickly that night, much to my dismay. It was all over Twitter. The Yankees' Phil Hughes tweeted, "I've watched it 20 times. I can't stop laughing."

"That was one of the funniest things I've ever seen," Francona said. "People still ask me about it today."

"Me, too," Arencibia said. "I get asked all the time, 'Give us your Kurkjian.'"

A couple of days later, the ESPN Bus Tour went to Port Charlotte, Florida, where then-Rays infielder Elliot Johnson followed Arencibia with another Kurkjian impersonation, which was also gleefully funny. When the Bus Tour went to Arizona, then-Brewers reliever Tim Dillard did his impersonation, only he bent down noticeably in order to get closer to my height. And when the Bus Tour went to Cubs camp in Mesa, pitcher Ryan Dempster,

who has done stand-up comedy and is a legitimate comedian, did
an impersonation of Harry Caray (it is so perfect) interviewing
me in my voice. Even I thought it was hilarious.

By the time I got to Giants camp that spring, at least a half-
dozen players had done my voice on *Baseball Tonight*. Former Giant
Will Clark, now a special instructor for the team, said to me,
"Those boys have made you look really stupid this spring. But
damn, it was funny."

Stupid? That describes every Tuesday at 2:30 p.m. during the
baseball season. That is my weekly spot on Scott Van Pelt's TV
show, which he hosts with Ryen Russillo. Van Pelt is one of the
funniest people on the face of the earth. It doesn't matter what
he says, he makes me laugh. His impersonations are tremendous,
he can do any dialect from any area of the country. He, like me,
is from Montgomery County, Maryland, and, like me, he spent a
lot of his youth going to Orioles games in Baltimore. That thick
Baltimore accent is unmistakable, and no one does it better than
Van Pelt. The long "oooooo" as in Jooooe Flacoooo or Leooooo
Mazoooone or Sixtooooo Lezcanooo is the signature Baltimore
accent.

So, every Tuesday for the last five years, Van Pelt and I talk
baseball for about ten minutes, then he makes some ridiculously
and purposely awkward segue, such as "Tim, do you like candy?"
or "I was thinking today about my favorite umpires from the
1980s," or "What's your favorite Sylvester Stallone movie?" By
that time, I am in full laugh, knowing what's coming next, a
punch line that features a long "oooooo" in it. "My favorite
Stallone movie," Van Pelt said, "is *Coooooobra*." Later that day,
Charles Barkley told Van Pelt on the air, "I can't believe *Cobra* is
your favorite Stallone movie."

"Charles," Van Pelt said, "you don't get the joke."

The listeners do, as they really seem to like the spot. They

e-mail Van Pelt every week with names that are certain to make
Kurkjian sound like a complete idiot on the air. At the urinal at
Busch Stadium in St. Louis one night, a total stranger looked at
me and said, "I'm Lieutenant Columbooooooo." In Pittsburgh
one day, a total stranger walked by me and said, "I'm from the
Congooooooo." Van Pelt laughs and says, "I want to stop doing
this. But I can't."

Stupid? Nothing compares to what happened to me at Miller
Park in Milwaukee in the summer of 2014. We were doing a
Nationals–Brewers game on *Monday Night Baseball;* I was the
on-field reporter that night. Mike McQuade, then our big boss
for baseball on ESPN, asked me to run in the Sausage Race that
night at Miller Park. I resisted, of course, but he insisted, so I
agreed to run. It was the worst decision I have ever made in my
life.

Stupid me, I just assumed since the Brewers had agreed to let me
run in the Sausage Race that they were going to rig it to let me
win. "No, we take the Sausage Race very seriously," said Drew
Olson of the Brewers. "We have a waiting list of people that want
to run in it: doctors, lawyers . . . this is a big deal at Miller Park."
I knew right then I was in trouble. But my trouble deepened
when the Brewers had me pick a suit in which to run. I was told
not to choose the chorizo—it was heavier than the others. So I
chose the hot dog.

"These suits are built for big guys," Olson told me. "And you
aren't very big."

Really?

"Do you have anything smaller, something in a breakfast sausage?" I asked.

No. I was going full frankfurter. I tried the suit on, and I
knew I was doomed. The suit was 9½' tall and unwieldy. I tried
briefly to run in it: it felt like I was running down the street holding

an opened patio umbrella in a wind storm while I was drunk. I am old and small; I knew I had no chance to win. The only question would be how spectacularly I would lose.

Before the game, I interviewed veteran Brewers radio broadcaster Bob Uecker, who might be the funniest person I have ever met in my life. He told me on national TV that I "should run in a sausage casing only. It will tighten you up. It will expose you, but so what? Who cares if you get arrested for indecent exposure as long as you win?" When I asked him if running this race meant the end of my career as a journalist, he said, "No, I think this is the start of something big for you, a road show—this is Vegas stuff. We could call it Slim Tim and His Sausage Casing Friends. What else do you want? What took you so long?"

A few minutes before the race, I met the four guys that would be running in the other costumes. They were age 16, 18, 23, and 28, meaning I was older than the three youngest combined. And all four were really big and really strong. I asked if they could slow down and let me win, and they quickly said no. "We keep track of who wins every night," one of them said. "All of us do other jobs in the park before and after the race, and whoever wins doesn't have to work the rest of the night. So, all of us have incentive to win."

I was nervous about making a fool of myself. It was an uneasy feeling being inside of a 9½' hot dog suit. I lost all my bearings, I lost all sense of time and space and direction. As we lined up for the race down the third-base line, Brewers third-base coach Ed Sedar, who knew I was the hot dog, began talking to me, and as I strained to hear him, the race began. I was facing the other direction because, for some unknown reason, I thought we were running the other direction. So, off to such a bad start, and running in a suit that was too big and too cumbersome, and running against professional pork products, I knew I was in big trouble. When I attempted to run fast, the height of the suit made it top-heavy, so I had to run while trying to hold the suit up, which made me look like a total dork.

I didn't fall, thankfully, but I finished last by a mile, clearly the most embarrassing night of my life. It was so bad, as I finally crossed the finish line a good fifteen seconds behind the rest, one of the organizers of the race yelled at me, "Hurry up, get off the field, the game is almost ready to start!" So I had to rush off the field so the sixth inning wouldn't begin with a hot dog in right field. My colleagues at ESPN—Sean McDonough, the play-by-play man, and Mark Mulder, the analyst—rightfully clobbered me after the race. All I had to cling to was the fact that it was not an athletic competition, it was a carnival act, and I had failed miserably.

After the game, I made the mistake of entering in the Brewers clubhouse.

"There he is," pitcher Kyle Lohse announced loudly, "the worst sausage ever!"

When I got back to the ESPN compound, I was greeted by big boss Mike McQuade, who led a standing ovation for me, then said in essence, "You were the star of the show because you were so terrible." And then, I'm not kidding, he gave me something to eat from the postgame spread, a staple from the fare at Miller Park, a Milwaukee favorite: bratwurst.

People I don't even know tell me how much they enjoyed my misfortune in the Sausage Race. I have covered baseball for more than thirty-six years, I have seen so many great games, interviewed so many great players, and yet, to some, I will be known for two things: a stupid impersonation by J. P. Arencibia, and an unbelievably stupid Sausage Race in Milwaukee.

But I wouldn't trade my experiences for anything. My time at
ESPN has been nothing but joy, especially spending time and
learning from my teammates, such as John Kruk, Aaron Boone,
Bobby Valentine, Terry Francona, Buck Showalter, and others.
And, thanks to Buck, whenever I meet a new young player, I
always check to see if he has a lot of freckles.

13. K's

Generation KKKKKKKKK

Cubs infielder Javier Baez, a supposed rising star, has tremendous bat and hand speed, and remarkable power. "The closest thing I've seen to Giancarlo Stanton," said catcher John Baker, a former teammate. Baez made his major league debut in 2014 and showed some of that power, yet displayed stunning ease in striking out, especially swinging and missing. Baez had 213 at bats and struck out 95 times, or more times than Babe Ruth struck out in any season of his career. Bill Buckner never struck out three times in a game in his twenty-year career, but Baez struck out four times in a game five times, two short of Richie Allen's major league record in 1968. Allen played 152 games that year, Baez played 52.

Welcome to the new generation of Major League Baseball—call it Generation K. In 2014, for the eighth consecutive season, the major league record for strikeouts in a season was demolished, reaching 15.41 strikeouts per game, nearly six more than the average in the 1980s. This conflagration of strikeouts is happening in part because major league pitching has never been better or more dominant, but also because there is an acceptance by hitters that striking out, no matter how many times, or when in the game, is no big deal. In 2015, 38 times did a team strike out 15 times, and win the game: That happened 22 times from 1900 to 1960 combined.

Hank Aaron never struck out 100 times in a season, but in 2014, 117 major league players struck out 100 times, more than there were from 1900 to 1963 *combined*. Of those 117, Mike Olt, Josh Willingham, George Springer, Brandon Barnes, and Juan Francisco did so in fewer than 300 at bats. Of those 117, 32 hit fewer than 10 homers, and Austin Jackson, Casey McGehee, Michael Bourn, Dee Gordon, and Jackie Bradley Jr. hit fewer than five. At least Bradley hit one, leaving Manny Lee in 1991 as the only player in major league history to strike out at least 100 times without hitting a homer.

Six times in history has a player struck out *200* times in a season, three times by infielder Mark Reynolds, whose record 223 strikeouts in 2009 are far more than the worst strikeout seasons of Ruth, Ted Williams, and Joe DiMaggio combined (197). The top-16 strikeout seasons by hitters have all come in this century. There have been forty-five 180-strikeout seasons in history, 39 of them in this century, and only three came before 1986.

"I hate it," said Nationals manager Dusty Baker. "It's embarrassing."

But to many hitters, it's not. To them, it's better than grounding into a double play. Mike Scioscia never struck out three times in a game, but in 2014, Phillies first baseman Ryan Howard recorded the 24th four-strikeout game of his career, breaking Reggie Jackson's record. But even Howard didn't do what A's infielder Adam Rosales did in 2013: he joined Graig Nettles in 1969 as the only players in the last 100 years to strike out four times in a game in which they didn't even play in the first nine innings. Also in 2013, Adam Dunn struck out in 31 consecutive games, six games longer than any other such strikeout streak in history. By comparison, the longest hitting streak of Dunn's career was only 12 games.

"Years ago, striking out was the Scarlet Letter," said Cubs manager Joe Maddon. "Now it doesn't matter."

The start of this strikeout craze came in 1986–87 when, among others, Rob Deer, Pete Incaviglia, Cory Snyder, Bo Jackson, and Jim Presley started playing every day; each struck out 150 times a year and hit 30 homers a year, and from then on it has been was okay to K. But now it is out of control. DiMaggio never struck out 40 times in any season in his career, but in April 2013, Chris Carter, Jay Bruce, and Mike Napoli all struck out 40 times.

Hall of Famer Frank Robinson said the worst season of his career (1965) was the only year that he struck out 100 times (he hit .296 with 33 homers and 113 RBIs, and was traded after the season). Hall of Famer Lou Brock sat out the final day of the 1970 season because he had 99 strikeouts, and didn't want to strike out 100 times again. Now, hitters reach 100 strikeouts at the All-Star break, if not well before. Dunn and the Orioles' Chris Davis hold the major league record for the fewest games—64—in a season to reach 100 strikeouts.

"I was joking with Adam in 2009 when I was striking out three times every game," said Davis. "He said he was genuinely upset that I was being sent back to the minors because he knew he'd be at the top of the strikeout list. I'm just glad others are jumping on the bandwagon."

Others? It's almost everyone.

"It's ridiculous," Dusty Baker said.

Mostly, it comes down to a different approach and attitude by hitters.

"No one chokes up anymore, no one tries to move the ball," Maddon said. "The bats are smaller and lighter, guys are swinging them as hard as they can in case they make contact. Years ago, guys would use a big bat, choke up, and try to move the ball. Not anymore. But you have to nurture that. You have to draft guys that don't swing and miss. When I was a hitting coach in the minor leagues, I used to use something called a B-Hack, which was less than your A-Hack. That plan consisted of choking up, looking for the ball away from you first, and looking for the fastball first. But hitters don't do that now."

Brady Anderson was a major league outfielder from 1988 to 2002. "When I first came up, I'd play right behind second base on Alan Trammell with two strikes because he became a slap hitter with two strikes," Anderson said. "I would do that with a lot of hitters with two strikes because a lot of them became slap hitters. [As a left fielder], I used to play Kenny Lofton right behind third base for his first four years in the league because he became a slap hitter with two strikes. Then he developed some power. By the end of my career, if I played shallow, just about everyone could hit it over my head with two strikes."

Chris Davis said, "When I was with the Rangers, they always preached that I had to put the ball in play. But I don't want to just put the ball in play. I want to do as much damage as I can. That's something that comes with being a power hitter: you are going to strike out."

The way the game has evolved, a strikeout is now treated as just another out, no worse than a weak ground ball to the second baseman, or a pop-out to third. And there is proof that you can win, at least in the regular season, even with a lot of strikeouts. In 2013, the A's won the AL West, winning 94 games, and their hitters set the AL record for most strikeouts in a season. The 2013 Braves won 96 games and the NL East despite joining the 2010 Diamondbacks as the only teams that struck out in at least

24 percent of their plate appearances. If a team wins, at least in the regular season, they can live with the K's.

"If a 3-4-5 hitter comes to the plate with one out and a runner at first, and he gets behind 0-2, and he shortens up and tries to put the ball in play, he might hit a ground ball that turns into a double play," John Baker said. "The next guy up might have gone deep, so he might have cost his team two runs. Do you think it's a good idea to ask Bryce Harper to swing at 50 percent? The same thing goes for Chris Davis and a bunch of other hitters. Asking Pablo Sandoval to not swing hard is ridiculous. It's ingrained. This is who they are as hitters. I'd rather him hit 30 homers with a lot of strikeouts than hit 14 with 60 RBIs, and not as many strikeouts. We can deal with the strikeouts as long as there is production."

Diamondbacks hitting coach Dave Magadan said, "I'm not a big fan of it, but the trade-off for driving the ball, for hitting the ball out of the ballpark, is accepting 180-190 strikeout seasons."

What really bothers veteran managers and coaches is that players are striking out far too often in key situations, such as a runner at third with less than two outs. They are striking out instead of moving the runner from second to third with none out. They are swinging on 0-2 the same way as they swing on 3-0. And, to some, they are swinging at too many pitches. Through 2014, the walk rate had decreased five years in a row, including by 4.2 percent in 2014.

"The high strikeout rate is due to the high chase rate: hitters are so determined to get a hit, they can't see the forest for a walk," Maddon said. "You have to take a walk, but so many guys are chasing balls out of the strike zone. They're not missing fastballs over the middle of the plate. They're missing elevated fastballs. They are chasing breaking balls, sliders, out of the strike zone. I mean, chasing truly bad pitches that are out of the strike zone."

In 2014, the Tigers and Yankees played a twelve-inning, no-walk game, the longest game without a walk since a thirteen-inning game in 1917. In 2013, the Phillies went four straight games without a walk for the first time since 1919–20. In 2013, Adam Wainwright of the Cardinals became the first ever to strike out 35 batters in a season before he walked a batter.

And yet there is even more evidence that hitters today are being *too* patient. Former manager Frank Robinson said, "I've never seen so many belt-high fastballs taken right down the middle on the first pitch. That might be the only pitch you get to hit." But that is the sabermetric way: take pitches, get on base, a walk is as good as a hit. In one recent season, the Astros, one of the leaders of the sabermetric revolution, had a rule in their minor league system that hitters were not allowed to swing at the first pitch of an at bat. As early as 2004, Dunn struck out looking an astounding 72 times: Ted Williams never struck out that many times in any single season. In 2013, Nationals catcher Kurt Suzuki went 113 consecutive plate appearances without swinging at the first pitch, claiming, "I like to see what a pitcher has that day," and said he wasn't afraid to hit behind in the count.

Dunn said, "It would be a lot harder to take if I didn't get on base a lot [he retired with the 40th most walks in history]. If I went to the plate and swung at the first three pitches every at bat, I would not strike out at all, but I wouldn't be helping my team win, either. I've tried to be more aggressive early in the count and eliminate strikeouts, but that didn't go too well, either. I guess you are who you are." Magadan agreed, saying, "It doesn't mean that if you run a count deep and still strike out, you've had a good at bat, but it's better than a three-pitch strikeout. We stress getting a good pitch to hit whether it's the first pitch of an at bat or the fifth pitch. If you attain that goal, but the at bat ends in a strikeout, at least you've taxed the pitcher a little, and you've given yourself a chance to walk. But for a pitcher to get you out, we want him to make three good pitches, not just one."

Still, John Baker says, "We have to be more aggressive as hitters. The common theory, the Billy Beane theory, the theory used by the Red Sox and Yankees, was to work a deep count, be patient, and get the starting pitcher out of the game. But in today's climate, you have to be more aggressive or you're going to strike out more often. We faced Jordan Zimmermann of the Nationals. We beat him, 2-1. He pitched eight innings and threw 87 pitches. We all went up there hacking, looking for the first fastball that we saw. Our thinking was, 'If he gets ahead in the count, there's a good chance we're going to strike out.'"

Zimmermann has great stuff. The pitching in the major leagues is spectacular on every level.

"It's the generation," John Baker said. "Players are bigger, better, and stronger than ever before, including pitchers. There's a better understanding of coaching today at every level: high school, college, and with special instructors for kids. They know how to pitch more effectively today. The riddle of how to get a guy out—change the eye level, changing speeds—isn't as difficult. The focus is clearer. Then you take away the rampant use of performance-enhancing drugs by hitters, and you get what we are seeing these days. Unless there's some sort of change, strikeouts are going to keep increasing every year."

In 2013, there were 13 starts of at least 12 strikeouts and no walks, which obliterated the major league record for such things: there were no such games in 1989, and only one in 1990. Also in 2013, the Phillies' Roy Halladay, who was pitching hurt, became the first pitcher ever to strike out nine in a start of 3⅓ or fewer innings. Alex Cobb, then the Rays' fifth starter, became the first pitcher to strike out 13 in an appearance of less than five innings.

"We just finished with the Nationals, then we got the Cardinals," John Baker said. "A new guy would come out of their bullpen, and we would look at his chart and say, 'Jeez, he's 96-100 mph with a 94-mph cutter.' Where in the hell are they finding these people?"

They arrive every day. The Mets' Matt Harvey arrived in 2013, and quickly became the only pitcher since 1900 to strike out 125 and allow fewer than 25 earned runs in his first 17 major league starts. Another Met, Jacob deGrom, arrived in 2014, and won the NL Rookie of the Year: he became the second pitcher ever to strike out the first eight batters of a game.

There are so many hard throwers today, so many pitchers with great secondary stuff, so many that have a slider or cutter or changeup or splitter or curveball to go with a 95-mph fastball. And most of them can throw a strike with three pitches, two of them off-speed pitches. They can throw most of those off-speed pitches when they are behind in the count.

"There are no more fastball counts anymore; 2-1 is a breaking-ball count today," said Orioles manager Buck Showalter. The Orioles charted every pitch from March 16 until the end of spring training one year, and found that 81 percent of 2-1 pitches are off-speed pitches.

"I get asked all the time, 'Are you looking for a pitch? Do you sit on a pitch?'" Davis said. "The answer is 'No, I don't.' You can't now because pitchers can throw all sorts of pitches for strikes in almost any count. There is a reason, you know, that no one hits .400 anymore."

In 2011, then-Cubs manager Dale Sveum was shocked to report that 50 percent of pitches thrown on 3-2 were off-speed, as opposed to his prime (the 1980s), when on 3-2 you got a fastball.

"If you are looking for something soft, and have to adjust to something up in velocity, that is impossible to hit," Maddon said. "Hitters are looking soft on 3-2. They can't adjust."

And it's not just the starters that have exceptional stuff, it's the relievers. The Royals made it to the 2014 World Series in part because the final three innings were dominated by a virtually unhittable trio of Kelvin Herrera (he throws a two-seam, sinking fastball at 101 mph), Wade Davis (he didn't allow his second extra base hit of the season until the final 10 days of the season), and closer Greg Holland (who, like the other two, overpowers hitters). In that World Series, the Giants had a relief pitcher named Yusmeiro Petit, who set a major league record that season for the most consecutive batters (46) retired.

"Every night," outfielder Lance Berkman said in 2013, "someone comes out of the bullpen throwing 95, and I've never even heard of him." Veteran infielder Willie Bloomquist said, "We're told by our coaches, 'Hey, we've got to get the starter out of the game and get into their bullpen.' And I am thinking, 'Why would we want to do that?'"

Dunn said, "Now you'll see three pitchers in the seventh, eighth, and ninth inning—and most of them are throwing 95 mph. For every crucial at bat I'll take late in a game, I'll always be facing the toughest lefty on the other team. That's why the strikeout rate is up."

And it's not just right-handers with power stuff, there are power left-handers everywhere: Clayton Kershaw, David Price, Aroldis Chapman, Matt Moore, and Chris Sale, to name a few.

"There are no more Jamie Moyers and Jim Parques," said former outfielder Vernon Wells, referring to two slightly built, softthrowing left-handers. "The lefties today are fire-ballers." A's first baseman Ike Davis's dad, Ron, played in the 1980s. "Back then," Ike said, "Ron Guidry was about the only left-hander that threw 95. Now they are everywhere."

John Baker said, "When I came up in 2008, the only power left-hander in a bullpen was Billy Wagner, who I was fortunate enough to face . . . or in my case, unfortunate to face. He was the only one. Billy Wagner was great, but now, you see more and more of them in that mold. Now there are Billy Wagners pitching the seventh, there are Billy Wagners as situational left-handers facing one batter in the eighth. That's how much pitching has improved."

Orioles reliever Darren O'Day is right-handed; he throws only in the upper 80s, not the mid-90s, but he's a strikeout pitcher, also, because he is so deceptive with his submarine delivery.

"When the hitters were just pounding the ball ten to twelve years ago, pitchers decided that they had to do something to strike hitters out, just to keep the ball in the park," O'Day said. "Maybe that's where the cutter came from. Pitchers decided that you can't let them make contact."

There is so little contact today, it's mindful of 1968, the Year of the Pitcher, a year so pitching rich, Major League Baseball lowered the mound in 1969 to help the offense. In 1968, the major league batting average was .237, compared to .251 in 2014. The league ERA was 2.98 compared to 3.74 in 2014. There were 1.84 homers per game in 1968 compared to 2.53 in 2014. It was so dominant, White Sox broadcaster Ken Harrelson, who hit 35 homers and had 109 RBIs that year, said, "It felt like every pitcher was right on top of you. It felt like they weren't 60 feet, 6 inches away, it felt like they were 40 feet away."

And yet, Harrelson now says, "I've never seen pitching like this—pitching is better than it has ever been. Those pitchers that year were awesome, something to behold, but in my fifty-five years in baseball, I've never seen as many good young pitchers as we have today. It's day after day after day. In 1968, there were four-man rotations, and you'd get two or three really good pitchers, but there was always one cookie in there. Today, you see a team for three or four days, and there are no cookies. And the pitchers are so big now. The biggest guy I ever faced was 6′ 6″, and that was [Dave] DeBusschere [who pitched for two years for the White Sox while also playing for the NBA Knicks]. One year against us, Tampa Bay started [Jeff] Niemann, who's 6′ 9″, and replaced him with Adam Russell, who's 6′ 8."

Harrelson paused.

"Back in '68, you would face the same guy [starting pitcher] three or four times every year," he said. "Back then, bullpens were places where bad starters went. But the game today is a battle of the bullpens. Also, Ted Williams used to say the hardest pitch to hit was the slider, but the cut fastball is the pitch that everyone has developed today. Today's guys are throwing in the 90s with movement, two-seamers, cutters. It's a bitch today."

It's a bitch all right, every night, for every hitter, especially for hitters such as Javier Baez.

14. OFFICIAL SCORING

No Runs, No Hits, All Errors

PROFESSIONAL BASEBALL DIDN'T get any smaller than in 1980 in Alexandria, Virginia. The Alexandria Dukes of the Class A Carolina League played their home games at Four Mile Run Park on the campus of Cora Kelly Elementary School, where classrooms served as the clubhouses. I covered that team as a 23-year-old for the *Washington Star* newspaper. *The Washington Post* occasionally sent a young guy named Peter Mehlman, who looked at me quizzically when I told him I wanted to make baseball writing a career, then said he planned to write and produce TV sitcoms in Hollywood. I never doubted that after the future writer/producer of *Seinfeld* called, in jest, in print, the Dukes' park "Three Mile Island Park," which ran in one edition of the *Post*.

Those days taught a young writer important lessons. 1. Don't operate a professional baseball team out of an elementary school. 2. Never joke about nuclear disasters unless your editor is aware of your humor, and closely reads your four-paragraph game story. 3. Given a choice, write *Seinfeld* episodes, not baseball. 4. It is really hard to be the official scorer.

I learned the last lesson painfully, often on a nightly basis, but never more than the night that Dukes pitcher Pete Garrity, a chunky right-hander out of Georgetown, unnecessarily jumped for a routine chopper to the mound. The ball bounced in and out of his glove so I scored it an error, which would have been no big deal except Garrity had a no-hitter going in the sixth inning. Well, fans began screaming at the press box, and a couple of visiting players glared my way, thinking, of course, that I was trying to protect Garrity's no-hitter. Exactly why I would do such a thing still remains a mystery to me, but it didn't matter because Garrity gave up a "legitimate" hit, several in fact, which got me off the hook. But it was my first understanding of how difficult it is being the guy sitting in that seat.

"When I did the job, people would come up to me and say, 'Oh, I could do that job, I know the difference between a hit and an error,'" said Phil Wood, who was one of the official scorers for Orioles games 1991–95. "But it's not that easy. It is a very hard job."

"The difference between what I'm doing, and what others are doing sitting at home, is like being on two different planets," said Bill Mathews, who was the baseball coach at Eckerd College for twenty-four years, and has been the primary scorer at Tampa Bay Rays games for the last seven years. "I'm sitting in the front row of the press box with a mike in my face, and when I turn that mike on, that is the voice of God, and I can't take it back. When you jump up in your living room and say, 'Oh, that's a base hit,' you are king of the kingdom. But I have several dozen experts in the press box who might not agree with my call. And if my job is so easy, why does the TV in front of me in the press box have a seven-second delay so I can watch a play again, and help me make the right call in twenty-five seconds?"

And it is thankless, the most thankless job in baseball, more thankless than being an umpire.

"An umpire has three other umpires for vindication; the official scorer is all by himself," said Phyllis Merhige, who coordinates official scorers as a senior vice president, club relations, for Major League Baseball. "It is a job where no good deed goes unpunished. You never make anyone happy as the official scorer. You always make someone unhappy."

Merhige employed eighty official scorers for the 2015 season, all independent contractors. Her goal is to rotate three scorers per team. Some work two or three games a year, others work eighty-one games a year. Most official scorers have some connection to the game, usually as a coach, an umpire, an ex-team employee, or an ex-member of the media. In the Australian professional baseball league, most of the official scorers are women, but there were no female official scorers in MLB in 2014. Man or woman, good or bad, they are evaluated yearly. Merhige said she has not renewed the contract of "several" scorers over the years.

"They have to be passionate about the game, they have to have an understanding of the rules and be able to interpret the rules," Merhige said. "They have to be willing to do a difficult, low-paying job. Official scorers are the custodians of the game, they are the official record of each game. It's a big deal. They have to pay attention, they have to be accurate. They must have a thick skin. They sit in the hot seat. That's a tough spot to be in."

Twenty years ago, the job paid $65 a game for about five hours' work if you arrived at the park an hour before a game; it takes three hours to play, then thirty to sixty minutes of paperwork after the game to make sure that the official box score is accurate. "That's why I stopped doing it. I spent so much time at the park, so much time on paperwork," Wood said. "I could have made more working at a High's store. But I wasn't in it for the money."

In 2014, official scorers were paid $160 per game (plus a free meal in the club's dining room, and, in some ballparks, reserved parking). They got a raise to $170 per game in 2015. When people say an ex–major league player should be the official scorer, pay is an issue.

"For $160 a game, I'd tell that to a former major leaguer as I was walking out the door," Mathews said, laughing. "I'm used to eating Subway subs on my lap in the front seat of the bus on the way back from Florida Southern. To me, $160 a game is good money. But when you've made $12,500 a game, you'd throw up your hands and say it's not worth it."

Still, Merhige says, "I would love to have a former major league player as an official scorer, but we've never had one since I took this job [in 2000]. A lot of that has to do with the pay, and the time commitment. I have begged the union to help me with ex-players. I can't find anyone. But I don't know if a player has the talent or patience to be a scorer."

Wood said, "Most former players don't even know the rules of the game. Most people don't know the rules of scoring. The first half of the official baseball rule book is about the rules of the game, the whole second half of the book is about the rules of scoring in the game. Most people never bother to read that. In the front of a scorecard you buy at the ballpark, it shows you how to keep score of a game. But scoring a game is a little more difficult."

Mathews said, "If you put a former big-league player up there, oh, my God, he would have a hard time stopping being a player. If you put a great defensive player up there, the incentives for major league infielders would be in big trouble because the scorer would expect that play to be made because *he* made that play. Wade Boggs could hit a bottle cap in a dark room. If he were the scorer, he'd think they should hit every pitch. If you put a former major league player up there for a seven-game series, it would be disastrous."

Former Orioles pitcher Dave Johnson served as an official scorer for one game twenty years ago.

"I have no idea how I wound up doing it," Johnson said. "Maybe it was because I had started doing some announcing. I didn't have any difficult calls, I didn't have any plays where I said, 'What do I do here?' I just remember it got a little tedious at the end checking the plate appearances and the at bats, and hoping that it all added up. But now that I'm at the ballpark every day, I watch the scorers work and say to myself, 'Hmm, what would I do there?' You can see a play one way, watch it again, see it another way, watch it again, and see it the way you saw it the first time. It can get a little crazy. It can get nerve-racking. I feel for the guys who are doing it because I've been in that chair before."

As for a former major leaguer understanding the intricacies of scoring a certain play, and determining complicated statistics, Mathews said, "It would be mind boggling. Earned runs? Oh, my God. That would be like explaining a calculus 3 problem. Explaining that to a former player would be like speaking in a foreign language, it would make no sense. Pitching coaches get it, but I've had some enlightening conversations with pitching coaches."

A scorer's attention to detail is crucial. He has to watch every play.

"You have to be zeroed in for three hours; that's not something that players had to do when playing," said Jim Henneman, who was an official scorer at Orioles games 1973–79 as a working member of the media, and has done it 1997–2015. "I tell people who think they do what I do this: You are observing the game, I'm watching the game."

Mathews said with a laugh, "Now I understand the purpose of

the seventh-inning stretch. It takes me exactly ninety seconds to run to the bathroom, get a Coke, then get back to my seat."

Johnson said, "It took me a little while to realize that I have to be watching everything, I can't turn away even for a second. This is a big deal. This is a big-league game, not a Little League game with your son. And you have to see it live. No matter how many times you see it on replay, you've got to see it live to understand where everyone was on that play."

"You have to get it right," Henneman said. "We are dealing with history here."

"We are the keepers of the game," Mathews said. "The responsibility is huge. Some guys get out of scoring because they can't handle the pressure and the money isn't worth it. I tell them all to check their ego at the door, they want the show to be about them, but it can't be. Some think it is all glitz and glamour, like you're hosting a segment on ESPN. But you're not: 50 percent of the people are going to be pissed at you whatever decision you make."

Most scorers agree that the hardest call is the hard-hit ball. Should it be caught, or was it too hot to handle?

"The most important part of scoring a game is to understand the degree of difficulty of a play," Wood said. "I hear people say all the time, 'That was a Little League play.' Really? The ball came off the bat at 98 mph. That's not happening in a Little League game. I hear people say all the time that this is a little boy's game played by grown men. It's not. It's a man's game being played by grown men. But everyone who has ever played on a church league softball team thinks that they have made that play. They haven't."

Henneman pitched for three years at Loyala College in Baltimore. He, as much as any writer I've ever met, understands what he is watching when he is watching a baseball game. "The speed of the ball is always the hardest play, it is always the most difficult call," Henneman said. "You have to understand the game, you have to have a feel for the game. Bill Stetka [another former official scorer for the Orioles] said it best when he once told me that with the speed of the ball, he's more surprised when they catch the ball rather than when they don't catch it. Most of us played the game along the way, but to equate where we played to what we are watching now is just wrong. You just can't do it."

Mathews played and coached the game. "I go down on the field before every game to see the pace of the ball," he said. "I think every official scorer should go down on the field to watch batting practice. They are hitting baseballs like they are Titleists. So, if I see a defensive player make a defensive play in a defensive manner—the ball is hit so hard, it puts him back on his heels—then I'm going to score that a hit. And slow-motion replay is tricky because it's not at game speed. If I go to replay, I like to see the play made at game speed."

One of Wood's most difficult calls came not on a hard-hit ball, but a topper hit out in front of the plate by Cal Ripken in the seventh inning of a game against the White Sox in 1991. Chicago catcher Ron Karkovice pounced on the ball, but threw over the head of the first baseman. "Some thought it would be a bang-bang play, but I thought it was a makeable play, he just rushed the throw," Wood said. "The rules of scoring say if you have replay, use it. So I did. I called it an error, and [Wilson] Alvarez went on to pitch a no-hitter. The next day, I got blistered by Cal Ripken Sr. [the Orioles third-base coach, and the father of Cal Ripken Jr.]. He said if that play had happened in Chicago, it would have been scored a hit. I told Cal, 'You have mistaken me for an Oriole fan.' He had no response for that. It's hard when you have to justify something that I thought was as plain as day."

Wood said it was "four or five years" before the controversy involving Alvarez's no-hitter went away. "The postscript is that after that game, I went to Ernie Tyler [then the Orioles umpire attendant who was in charge of the baseballs] and asked for a ball from that game," Wood said with a laugh. "He gladly gave me one. Years later, when Alvarez went to the Rays [in 1998], I asked [the Rays director of public relations] Rick Vaughn if he could get Alvarez to sign it for me. He was happy to. He signed it, 'Phil Wood, I couldn't have done it without you.' That's *not* what I wanted him to write. I told Rick that I was surprised that Wilson remembered me, and Rick told me, 'Oh, he knows you well.'"

Mathews has been the official scorer for no-hitters thrown by Matt Garza and Edwin Jackson. "I didn't have any difficult calls, but in Garza's no-hitter, in the ninth inning, a batted ball knuckled on its way to [left fielder Carl] Crawford," said Mathews. "I watched his knee buckle and his head tilt, and I thought, 'Oh, God, I am going to be on *SportsCenter* tomorrow morning.' But Crawford went down to one knee, and caught the ball."

Mathews had a one-hitter by R. A. Dickey in which the only hit was a topper down the third-base line by the first hitter of the game, B. J. Upton. "He beat the play by five strides," Mathews said. "After the game, Rick Vaughn came to me and said that ESPN and MLB.com wanted to talk to me, but he wouldn't let them. I asked, 'About what?' He said, 'The only hit of the game was a topper in the first inning.' Well, that is not a problem. That's a hit. No-hitters are tough. When I am in one, by the seventh inning, I start calling pitches in the game to distract myself from worrying, 'What if there's a topper?'"

A hit is a hit no matter when it comes, most scorers say; there's no logic to the first hit having to be a "clean" hit. "I always think about the story about Roberto Clemente," Henneman said. "He was going for his 3,000th hit. In his second-to-last game of that [1971] season, he hit a topper down the third-base line. It should have been scored a hit, but the scorer didn't want Clemente's

3,000th hit to be a dribbler, so he called it an error. The next day, the last day of the season, Clemente got his 3,000th hit [it was his last hit. Clemente died in a plane crash two months later]. But what if he hadn't gotten a hit the last day?"

Actually, the Pirates had three more games that season. Clemente didn't bat in any of them, but homer-ism by official scorers has long been a concern in Major League Baseball. For years and years, beat writers that covered the team often acted as the official scorer. The most famous case of homer-ism came on June 17, 1941, in what would be game 30 of Joe DiMaggio's 56-game hitting streak. DiMaggio was struggling at the time, with only one hit in each of his last three games. Johnny Rigney was pitching for the White Sox; DiMaggio had faced him 15 times during the streak with only four hits. Rigney had retired DiMaggio three times that day, and in the fourth at bat, DiMaggio hit what looked to be a routine grounder to shortstop Luke Appling. The ball took a hop off Appling's chest, caromed off his shoulder and into left field. Several observers said that Appling had misplayed the hop and, at worst, could have kept the ball in front of him and made the play.

The official scorer that day was the writer Dan Daniel, who covered the Yankees. He scored it a bad-hop single, which came as no surprise to some because Daniel had once written a column titled "My Friend, the Yankee Clipper." Wood said, "I talked to Shirley Povich [a Hall of Fame sportswriter] about that play, and he said the ball rolled up Appling's arm. Daniel and DiMaggio were buddies. Shirley told me that people who saw that game thought it should have been an E-6."

A lot has changed in official scoring since the Daniel/DiMaggio controversy. At some point in the 1980s, newspapers chose not to allow their writers to be official scorers because it was a conflict of interest, and it could affect their coverage of the team.

In theory, if a scorer gave a player an error, angering the player, the player therefore might stop talking to the writer, putting him at a distinct disadvantage against the other writers covering the team.

It was not uncommon for years and years for players, coaches, and managers to call the press box after a game, or during a game, to argue an official scorer's call. "[Then-Angels manager] Doug Rader called me after a game after I gave his shortstop, Donnie Hill, an error because he dropped a line drive hit right at him," Wood said. "He said, 'I don't know if you noticed from up there, but that ball knuckled. It's was like trying to hit a good knuckleball from Charlie Hough.' I told him, 'Doug, I can't give your shortstop a passed ball.' He laughed and said, 'Well, I guess you got me on that one.' And that was it."

Sometimes, scorers would go speak to a player after a game to discuss a call he had made. But now that has changed: the scorer needs the permission from the club's PR staff to speak to a player about a play. And players, managers, and coaches are not allowed to call the press box to argue a call. And the scorer, who often used to sit with the PR staff in the middle of the press box, is now sequestered in a booth so as not to be harassed by anyone.

For the last four years, MLB has held a two-day seminar, usually in February, in which one official scorer from each team is invited to discuss his job and view video. Joe Torre, MLB's executive vice president of baseball operations, speaks to the scorers at those meetings. MLB has formed the Official Scorer's Advisory Commission, a three-man panel that includes Mathews, Ron Roth, an official scorer from Cincinnati, and Stew Thornley, who scores Twins games. They review videos, discuss plays, and share ideas. MLB has also developed an electronic bulletin board in which scorers, at any time, can share videos and decisions.

"One official scorer told me that before we did this, he felt like he was out on an island all by himself," said Merhige. "Now he has a place to talk. He knows everyone else has the same issues he does. No two plays are ever alike, but we are trying to get some uniformity."

Mathews runs a portion of the seminar.

"I don't see it just as a hit or an error, I call it an athletic read," Mathews said. "Where was the fielder when the play began? At what angle was he coming from? What was the angle of his glove when the ball went in? What was the angle of his arm when he threw? Where was his release point? For outfielders, from what direction did the ball come? What was the three-point arc of that fly ball? As a coach, we watch these things when we evaluate a player, and we can do it in three seconds. So, using an athletic read, I am a lot more comfortable making 96 percent of the calls . . . but then there are the other 4 percent."

But how can an official scorer who didn't play the game as Mathews did make an athletic read?

"That is the purpose of the seminar," he said. "I can teach it to a scorer even if the most competitive thing he's ever done is backgammon. I am a teacher. I can show them what to look for. I can teach without preaching. The seminar, in every way, is an invaluable help for scorers. We teach them there is no right way or wrong way, every single play is different from every other play. It gives them a subconscious level of comfort that other guys are having the exact same issues that they are. It can get pretty lonesome sitting up there."

The biggest change in the scoring system was collectively bargained three years ago, and is now part of the new Basic Agreement. If a player, coach, or manager has a complaint about an official scoring call, he has seventy-two hours to send it to MLB offices for review: every team has an operations person in charge of being a liaison to Torre, who looks at all plays under review. In 2014, Torre reviewed 366 plays, roughly 100 more than in 2013, and roughly 200 more than in 2012. Merhige said Torre "usually reverses about one-third of them."

Henneman said, "It is much better this way. It takes the PR staff out of the equation. Anything that can avoid confrontation with players and coaches, I'm 100 percent behind that."

Merhige said that scorers that have their calls changed "usually accept it, but say they respectfully disagree with Mr. Torre. Some are upset. They just want to get it right. I had a scorer quit, not because of the system, or that calls were overturned, but he got sick of one of his players complaining all the time, and always asking for one of his plays to be reviewed."

Mathews said, "If my decision gets to Joe Torre, I must have done a good job if a man of his stature is reviewing my decision. I wouldn't care if he reviewed every decision I made as long as we get it right. That's all we care about and should care about is getting the call right."

In 2014, Torre famously changed a scoring call made by Steve Weller, one of the official scorers for the Texas Rangers. On May 9, Texas' Yu Darvish had a no-hitter going with two outs in the seventh inning when Boston's David Ortiz hit a towering fly ball to right field. Rangers second baseman Rougned Odor, who was playing his second game in the major leagues, was playing a good 80 feet deeper than he usually plays because of the famed Ortiz shift. The ball clearly was a catchable ball, but the shift complicated the matter. Rangers right fielder Alex Rios wasn't used to having a second baseman that close to him, and Odor wasn't used to playing that deep, or being that close to the right fielder. Neither confused fielder came close to catching the ball, but

Weller scored it an error. The backlash was immediate and furious: some felt Weller was protecting Darvish's no-hitter.

Darvish gave up a "clean" hit to Ortiz in the ninth inning, but the damage had been done to official scorers everywhere. They are never lauded for making a good call, they are only blasted for making a controversial call. Several days later, Torre reversed the error to a hit.

"Scorers kick that play around all the time: on a ball hit like that, that ball has to be caught," Henneman said. "Did he not catch it because of the sun, the lights, the wind, the shift? We all agree that there has to be an error on that play . . . until you give someone an error."

Plays such as that remind me of my days as an official scorer for the Alexandria Dukes in 1980. They remind me of my days as a teenager when all I loved was baseball, but I was a terrible writer, and I had to find a way to stay in the game once my high school playing career was over. So, I decided that I wanted to be what I called "an official official scorer." However redundant that might have been, I am glad that I learned, at least on some level, how to write because I wouldn't want to be an official scorer. It is too hard, too much pressure, and too much time, and if I worked all 81 games, I'd make $13,770 a year.

15. STATE OF THE GAME

Baseball Heaven in Hazleton

HOPE COMES FROM all places, and on a freezing night in December 2014, it came from Hazleton, Pennsylvania. Joe Maddon, the new manager of the Cubs, held his annual fund-raiser for his hometown. I had the honor of serving as the moderator of a Q&A with Maddon and Cal Ripken Jr., who donated $180,000 to the Hazleton cause. It was a dream matchup for me, a layup, two of the most astute and articulate baseball guys in the same room for one hour. One hundred people, at $1,000 per person, attended. About ten minutes into the session, when the subject detoured to the secret world of relaying signs, Maddon said he knew how Ripken signaled to the catcher what pitch to throw, then that sign was sent to the pitcher.

Maddon stood up, sifted imaginary dirt with his right foot, and said, "You did it like this, right?"

Then Ripken stood up and said, "No, that's what I wanted you to think. That was a fake sign."

And then Ripken and Maddon went on for fifteen minutes with as compelling a lesson as you will ever see on the undercover realm of relaying signs. Ripken, using virtually every part of his body, showed how he signaled for a slider, a changeup, a fastball on the inside part of the plate, a fastball away, etc. The two great baseball men took a hundred people inside the game to a place where only the privileged are allowed, a place where Ripken usually allows no one. As this wonderful riff was taking place, I looked at the crowd. There wasn't a sound in the room, all eyes were on Ripken and Maddon, a hundred people totally dazzled.

"Okay," Ripken said to the crowd, "what is the sign for the slider?"

One hundred people tapped their nose.

"Curveball?" Ripken said.

One hundred people rubbed their chin.

And when the little quiz was over, I said to the crowd, "Ladies and gentlemen, that is baseball."

As long as the likes of Joe Maddon and Cal Ripken Jr. have anything to do with the game, there is hope for the game. There is always hope for the game. Even with relative sagging attendance and TV ratings, with complaints about the pace of the game, questions about instant replay, controversies involving the Hall of Fame and PED users, and a generation of players that are so talented, but have a troublesome sense of entitlement, there is hope for the game on every level, even without icons Mariano Rivera and Derek Jeter.

There is hope in the new faces of baseball. Mike Trout is Mickey Mantle come back to life, complete with a naive, aw-shucks countenance that is endearing, and with numbers that were even better than the Mick's through three full seasons. The smile on Trout's face during the 2014 All-Star Game was unmistakable, especially after he and his idol, Jeter, teamed up to produce the game's first run. And when Trout was removed after five innings, Jeter went to him in the dugout and said, "How old are you, 22?

And you're only playing five innings? What's wrong with you?"
And then he gave Trout a gigantic hug.

No pitcher has ever had numbers through age 27 better than
Clayton Kershaw's, but Kershaw comports himself even better
than he pitches, which is encouraging for the game. There are
fresh faces and remarkable talents everywhere, from Giancarlo
Stanton, Andrew McCutchen, and Jose Altuve, to World Series
hero/farmer Madison Bumgarner, who is so unaffected by the
fame the game can bring, he gave his wife a calf for her birthday.

Now all we have to do is keep the players healthy. In 2014,
thirty-seven pitchers underwent Tommy John surgery to repair
injured elbows. Exactly why this epidemic is happening is unclear, but Dr. Tom House, a former major league pitcher and
pitching coach, and a man who knows more about the throwing
of a baseball than anyone else alive, told me, "Our kids today are
pitching too much and not throwing enough. When we were
kids, we threw rocks and tennis balls and footballs and everything, all weights and sizes, from all different angles. That's how
you strengthened your arm. Now, our kids are throwing a baseball
from a mound twelve months a year, using the exact same motion. That's how you hurt your arm. It's too much. Put the ball
down. Play another sport. And give your arm a rest."

Even when today's players are healthy, they are far from perfect.
They are bigger, stronger, and faster than ever, but they are not
necessarily better because they don't understand the subtle nuances of the game as, say, Ripken did. In spring training 2014, a
young Seattle Mariner was on first base with one out in the
eighth inning. There also was a runner on third base. Andy Van
Slyke, the first-base coach, told the young runner on first that since
the Mariners were ahead by 10 runs, and it was late in a spring
training game, if there was a potential double-play ground ball,
it was not necessary for the runner to go hard into second base to

break up the double play and potentially get himself or someone else hurt. So, Van Slyke instructed, just peel off into right field. The next batter struck out. Now there were runners on first and third with two out. The batter hit a ground ball deep in the hole to the shortstop, his only play was at second, and it would have been close, but the clueless young runner at first figured the same rules applied. So instead of running all the way to second base, likely beating the throw, he peeled off into right field.

"What was that?" Mariners manager Lloyd McClendon, astonished, asked Van Slyke.

Van Slyke shook his head and said, "I have no idea."

There is hope in the new commissioner, Rob Manfred, who followed Bud Selig, who might be the most influential, progressive commissioner in baseball history. Under Selig, massive changes occurred, including two Wild Card teams, interleague play, and instant replays, but none bigger than revenues in the game rising from $1.8 billion in 2004 to $9 billion in 2014. New TV deals on the national and club level have greatly boosted operating capital, which has helped the competitive balance of the game. The last few years, small-market teams such as the Rays, A's, Royals, and Pirates have made the playoffs because they smartly use their assets, and because they have more assets than ever.

Manfred was handpicked by Selig and, like Selig, he isn't some dashing figure with a natural presence about him; he doesn't inspire confidence at first glance, but Manfred is a brilliant guy who understands the inner workings of baseball because he has been an integral part of the game for the last fifteen years. Manfred may have the sheepish look of an overworked accountant, but make no mistake, he has a steel spine: it was Manfred, we're told, even more than Selig, who wanted to pursue and punish steroid users. That's not to say performance-enhancing drugs are gone from the game, but Manfred, from all indications, will make sure everything possible will be done so they don't re-emerge.

There is, however, still the problem with what to do with PED users and the Hall of Fame. I have been a Hall of Fame voter for twenty-six years, it is my greatest privilege as a writer, and I still don't know how to handle the PED issue. If you don't vote for the steroid guys, you are called a hypocrite and a sanctimonious fraud. If you do vote for the steroid guys, you are soft on PED, and condone cheating. I voted for Barry Bonds and Roger Clemens each of their first three years on the ballot because I am not comfortable as the moral arbiter, and it seems to me that cheating has been going on in baseball for 150 years, especially during the Steroid Era. It seems to be that a lot of players were doing it; there was this tacit agreement in the game that you can do this, no one will know, no one will get caught.

Now MLB has tossed this issue of the Hall of Fame into the laps of the writers and said, "You figure this out." Well, we're not good enough, and neither is anyone else. It's too difficult and complicated. It's time for a nationwide discussion with the leaders of the Hall of Fame, the writers, the commissioner, the union, and some current Hall of Fame players to determine what to do about this issue, and determine what Cooperstown actually is. Is it a museum that chronicles the history of the game, or is it a sacred place where only a select few are allowed? It's not clear to me. Some have suggested a separate wing in the Hall for steroid users, or special notations on the plaques of PED guys, but no suggestion has been sufficient. This is a cumbersome issue that is not going away, and will only get worse when Manny Ramirez, Alex Rodriguez, and others are eligible for the Hall.

Manfred has other issues, including the pace of the game, something he aggressively took on soon after replacing Selig in January 2014. Orioles manager Buck Showalter has told me many times, "There are only two sets of people that complain about the time of game: umpires and the media, because they have to work longer. No one is sitting in the stands saying the game is taking too long." Indeed. But MLB, led by Red Sox co-owner Tom Werner, is worried "about all the dead time in the game." Eventually, MLB will have a pitch clock, which will require pitchers to deliver the ball in a specified amount of time, perhaps 20 to 25 seconds. The dead time to which Werner refers is (among others) Josh Beckett, now retired, taking 50, 53, 56 seconds between pitches. A pitch clock likely will need at least two years of trial service in the minor leagues to see if it works, and to prepare the next wave of pitchers and hitters to be ready to hit or pitch sooner than they are now.

There is hope with baseball's new breed of young, brilliant, aggressive general managers. The days of a former player running a team are mostly over. The game is now being run by Ivy League–educated GMs. "It's not just that they are smart," said ESPN analyst Jim Bowden, a former GM for the Reds and Nationals. "It's that they have surrounded themselves with six other really smart guys, and get together in a room and figure out how they can make a trade. With seven smart guys working together, things happen." We saw that at the 2014 winter meetings when Andrew Friedman, who now runs the Dodgers baseball operation, overhauled the team in twenty-four hours, and also saved money doing it.

Two weeks later, new Padres GM A. J. Preller remade his team in two days, turning it from irrelevant into something they could build on in the NL West. Preller went to Cornell, he is wicked smart, he has a photographic memory, and he is wildly competitive, something I've seen too many times playing basketball with and against him in spring training every year. It didn't matter the size of the game, 2-on-2 with no one waiting, or

5-on-5 with 10 people waiting, he would tear your throat out before he would allow you to win. And now, it appears, he has taken that same attitude to the GM job, which, in every way, is good for baseball.

There are problems in baseball, but Selig left the game in good shape, and in good hands. Almost everyone, especially the players, are thriving financially, and the level of play, even with some players who have no idea how to play the game, is exceptionally high. The games are great, as they've always been. The final day of the 2011 season—three crucial games, all televised on ESPN, all decided within about ten minutes of each other—was, by any measure, the greatest day in the history of regular season baseball. The postseason has been spectacular in this century, but especially in this decade. Every October night, something happens that you weren't expecting, or had never seen, and might never see again.

The game still has its magic, which we saw in that warm meeting hall on that freezing night in Hazleton, Pennsylvania, with Maddon and Ripken. Maybe that sort of high-level discussion happens between two NBA players or two NFL players, but I doubt it. Maybe the fans of other sports get the same mesmerized look on their face when they are privy to such private, secretive explanations of other sports, but I doubt it. I looked in the eyes that night of those one hundred fans, the ones that sat in glorious silence, and their eyes all said the same thing.

Baseball is the best game.

Acknowledgments

IT WAS SUCH a pleasure writing about the game I love. For this, I have several people to thank.

I want to thank my beautiful mom, the aptly named Joy, who taught me to love words, and inspired me to write. She learned to appreciate baseball living in our house, a house in which baseball was the only language spoken. My brothers, Andy and Matt, are in the baseball Hall of Fame at the Catholic University, and no one had a better feel for the game than my late father, Jeff. He would jokingly tell his three boys that he was a better hitter than Joe DiMaggio because, at age 70, he *was* a better hitter than Joltin' Joe, who refused to play in Old-Timers Games because, like Bob Cousy, he didn't want anyone to remember him as a broken-down old player; he wanted to be remembered for streaking through the outfield to make a great catch, or tearing a hole in the sky with a line drive.

So for Christmas 1989, I had made for my father a license plate frame that read: "Better Hitter Than Joe DiMaggio." My dad died in 2003, and soon after, my mom swapped her car for his. One day she came home, totally confused, and told me that a motorist had rolled down his window at a red light, and yelled at her, "But I bet you're not a better hitter than Ted Williams!'" My mom naively asked me, "What do you think he meant by that?"

I want to thank my editor at St. Martin's Press, Marc Resnick, for taking such good care of the words in this book. I want to thank George Will, who, several times a year, has encouraged me to write another book, then volunteered to write the foreword for this book. My lunches with George and Charles Krauthammer a few times a year are a highlight for me despite, intellectually, feeling like a complete dope sitting next to them. I want to thank Dan Shaughnessy for being my mentor since I was 21, when I loved the game and had no idea what to do with it. I want to thank my wife, Kathy, for urging me to write another book, and our children, Kelly and Jeff, for supporting Dad and his, at times, obsessive love for the game and for his work. I want to thank my brother Matt for helping me take care of Mom so I had time to write, be it in the middle of the day or the night.

And I want to thank my nephew, Brett Townsend, who read my last book, *Is This a Great Game, or What?* That was a collection of the favorite stories that I had accumulated over the first twenty-five years of my career as a baseball writer. It was, hopefully, a fun, easy, entertaining look at the game, no heavy lifting, not the rants of some pedantic little twit. Brett was 13 when he read my book. Soon after, he was asked in English class to compare and contrast two pieces of literature, so he picked my book and—I am not making this up—*The Odyssey* by Homer, which was written in 800 B.C.

Sadly, I never read *The Odyssey,* and I don't know anything about Homer, but I know Homer Bush, who hit 11 career home runs for the Yankees and Blue Jays, and I know Homer Bailey, who has thrown two no-hitters for the Reds. He also bears a striking physical resemblance to actor Christian Bale. "My mom told me that," Bailey said. "She said, 'You know you look like the guy that played Batman.' He's good-looking. I'm okay with that."

My cousin, Julie Townsend, was not okay with her 13-year-old comparing and contrasting the mindless, harmless work of a dinky little baseball writer to that of a Greek philosopher who lived around the time of the Trojan Horse. To her credit and my amusement, she acknowledged that there are Homers in each book, but softly suggested to her son that "maybe we can find something more comparable" than *The Odyssey* and Uncle Tim's book.

So they did. Still, my life has been a baseball odyssey, one I have shared with many. I see it every day, at every ballpark that I visit, everywhere I go. At the Cincinnati airport in 2014, a young couple approached me and explained that they had celebrated their third wedding anniversary by going to the Great American Ballpark: every year, on their anniversary, they plan to visit a new ballpark. Such annual journeys only happen in baseball.

At a speaking engagement a couple of years ago, a 10-year-old boy came up to me, and instead of asking me what was my favorite team, or who was going to win the World Series, he asked me, "What did you think of the Jesse Chavez trade?" Jesse Chavez? At Busch Stadium in St. Louis, I met a family—a dad, mom, and three grown-up daughters—that go to most of the Cardinal games: the mom drives a Volkswagen bug that looks like a baseball, complete with seams that cover the car. At my hometown Safeway in 2012, a neighbor lady tackled me in the frozen food aisle to breathlessly tell me, "I love baseball now! I'm hooked! I watch the Nationals every night! I got it! Now I know how you feel!"

This is why I cover baseball, for these people, for the people who get it, or want to get it someday. They are why I wrote this latest book. Brett Townsend is 20 now, and I fully expect him, in English class at UC Santa Barbara, to compare and contrast two pieces of literature: *I'm Fascinated by Sacrifice Flies* and *The Iliad* by Homer.

About the Author

Tim Kurkjian has been a baseball writer, reporter, analyst, and host at ESPN for more than eighteen years. A senior writer at *ESPN The Magazine* and ESPN.com, he has been a regular on *Baseball Tonight* and *SportsCenter* for its entirety.